BILL HUEBSCH

DREAMS AND VISIONS

PASTORAL PLANNING FOR LIFELONG FAITH FORMATION

The definitive guide

TWENTY THIRD 23rd
PUBLICATIONS

Dedication

Bishop Ray Lucker
Teacher, Friend, and Co-worker
in the Vineyard

Twenty-Third Publications
A Division of Bayard
One Montauk Avenue, Suite 200
New London, CT 06320
(860) 437-3012 or (800) 321-0411
www.23rdpublications.com

ISBN 978-1-58595-638-8
Library of Congress Catalog Card Number: 2007930686
Printed in the U.S.A.

Contents

Acknowledgments

Parts of Chapter 2 have appeared in other publications, including various magazines or web articles over the past ten years, as well as in *The Pastor's Guide to Whole Community Catechesis* (New London: Twenty-Third Publications, 2004). They are edited and expanded here.

All Scripture uses are taken from *The Catholic Youth Bible* (Winona: St. Mary's Press, 2000).

I am indebted to William McDonough, Assistant Professor of Theology at The College of St. Catherine in St. Paul, Minnesota, for permission to use portions of the research he did into the life and contributions of Bishop Ray Lucker. "Raymond A. Lucker (1927-2001): Bishop-herald of catechesis for conversion in an adult church" (March 2007).

The "Living Christ" retreat discussed in Chapter 5 and offered in English and made available on www. PastoralPlanning.com as a reproducible resource, also appeared earlier in the *Handbook for Success in Whole Community Catechesis* (New London: Twenty-Third Publications, 2004). It has been revised and updated in this version. It is also available in Spanish on the web site.

Parts of Chapter 7 on the "50-50 Partnership Agreement" have been published previously in *Whole Community Catechesis in Plain English* (New London: Twenty-Third Publications, 2002). They are edited and expanded here.

In Chapter 8, a section is reproduced verbatim from the U.S. Bishop's Pastoral Plan for Adult Faith Formation,

The "Question of the Week" resource for breaking open
the Word, which is provided as a reproducible resource
at www.PastoralPlanning.com, appeared earlier in *Whole
Community Catechesis in Plain English.* It has been edited
and expanded there.

I am indebted to Jim Collins, author of *Good to Great*
(New York: HarperCollins, 2001), whose insights into
business, presented in that book are applied here with
certain adaptations directly to Catholic parish pastoral
planning.

Introduction to
DREAMS AND VISIONS

Did you ever know someone with dreams and visions for the church? There are many people who have them, and I'll bet you're one! If so, you take your place alongside women and men of all kinds whose dreams and visions have been shaping the church for centuries.

Pope John XXIII had dreams and visions for the church. They were taken up and given lofty expression at the Second Vatican Council. His dreams led others to dream with him, and after him both Popes Paul VI and John Paul II had visions as well. The popes, of course, are only servants of the church, the People of God. And the People of God have dreams and visions, too. You'll be reading about all of these dreamers in this book.

This book is a guide to help you move in the direction of the dreams and visions that you have for your parish, but the writer here doesn't ever promise that you will actually get there! As you will see in this book, the process of turning dreams and visions into specific programs and processes, a task known in the church as pastoral planning, never actually comes to an end.

GOOD OR GREAT?

In the introduction to his powerful book, *Good to Great,* (New York: HarperCollins, 2001), Jim Collins wrote, "Good is the enemy of great. And that is one of the key reasons why we have so little that becomes great."

He's so correct! And for Catholic parishes, this is a powerful wake-up call. The church is filled with "good" parishes: The liturgies are planned. The education programs use a nice-looking book. Some of the people take an active role in parish leadership and ministry. The collections pay the bills for the most part. People can get their children baptized without too much hassle. The second-grade students receive their first communions, as they do every year. Couples getting married go through their routine of meetings. Lent comes and Easter follows, and sometime around Pentecost, things slow down for summer. It's a "good" parish.

But can we really afford to keep focusing only on being good? The world is bigger than that in every direction, more challenging and more dynamic. And it needs the message we have to bring. We have, after all, the secret of the Reign of God, and we need to be more than merely "good" to announce that. We need to move toward becoming *great!*

SETTING THE CHURCH ON FIRE!

In a great parish, the liturgy will not only be planned, but a team of leaders will also plan how to increase from mediocre to fantastic both 1) the level of participation and 2) the sense of welcome. In a great parish, the education process will not only use a good textbook, but over time a team of leaders will plan ways to provide faith formation for *all* members, including adults, using the textbook as a springboard. In a great parish, not only will there be some people actively involved, but a team of leaders will plan ways to gradually engage more and more people in parish life, by lighting a fire in people's hearts through encounters with Christ. In a great parish, not only will the collections pay the bills, but a

We want to set the church on fire!

team of leaders will gradually see collections rise to the point where the parish is able to afford more, not only for itself but also for the whole community. In a great parish, not only will children and young people celebrate the sacraments, or couples prepare to marry, but a team of leaders will plan how to place those preparing for sacraments in the context of the whole community, and the catechumenate will be the inspiration and empowerment behind it all. In a great parish, catechists and teachers will be in ongoing formation, creating a spiritual community at the hearts of our schools and parishes.

And here's the Core Work to be done: in a great parish, a team of leaders will gradually build up a process by which members have either 1) an initial encounter with Christ and his life-changing presence or 2) deeper communion with him through retreats and encounters. In a great parish, people will have a way through which that conversion can be sustained for life, through Faith Gatherings and other means. Little by little in a great parish, a fire will be lit. Little by little, a team of leaders will help move the parish forward, not merely to repeat this year what they did last, but also to lead in a consistent direction over a long period of time. They will build momentum gradually until one day, a few years from now, everyone will stop and look back and say, "Gosh, we're really a *great parish*, aren't we?"

Great parishes aren't built by simply following after the latest pastoral trends. They aren't built in one or two or three years. They aren't built by entrepreneurial pastors who fight the chancery and do their own thing. Even if that looks good for a while, in the end when that pastor is gone, the parish will suffer implosion. It takes a lot of effort and a team of modest yet driven leaders to shift from being good to being on the road to greatness, as Jim Collins reminds us in his book. There is no one plan or one action or one program to adopt that can make a parish great. But there is a direction, and that direction is set by the church itself, as you will read in these pages.

So rather than suggest big new programs to implement, *Dreams and Visions* suggests moving in the constant direction of lifelong faith formation by establishing a pattern of growth, step-by-step, little by little. *Dreams and Visions* suggests a strong plan of formation for the whole community, but it also cautions you not to run off in several directions at once. The Core Work (the "Hedgehog Concept" in Jim Collin's book) is quite simple and we keep returning to it constantly. It's the concept that comes to us from the popes and bishops, but also directly from the Gospel. And that Core Work, of course, is the center point of *Dreams and Visions*. Every single dimension of pastoral planning suggested here leads always to and from this core: to help people experience an initial encounter with Christ, or to grow into deeper communion with God, or to turn one's heart toward Christ, or to go through a conversion, or to be part of the "new evangelization" described by John Paul II. However you name it, there is one central vision here: *Help people deepen their communion with Christ and you will light a fire in your parish!* That is the dream and vision of this book.

Through discipline and consistency, we will gradually build up our good parishes into great ones by growing the number of people who are on fire with the love of Christ and each other. Once the momentum begins, the movement will sustain itself. All the parish leaders have to do is stoke the fire and keep out of the way.

We sometimes settle for so little as parish workers and members. We're willing to accept the modest goal of balancing a budget or not making anyone angry in the parish. What is that about? It's about safety and security. But growing the parish requires risk, danger, and maybe even our very lives. It requires us to go out on a limb. It requires us to do what Pope John XXIII did when he was inspired to call Vatican II. The idea of a council, he later said, appeared to him "like a flash of heavenly light." He trusted that flash, and in his own modest yet determined way he changed the course of history and all our lives as well. (Clearly he was a Level 5 Leader as described by Collins in *Good to Great*.)

A FLASH OF HEAVENLY LIGHT

Now the task is upon us. Don't settle for being merely a good parish. Don't pass from one year to the next repeating the same pleas for engagement on the part of your members. Don't sit back and wait for the ones coming after you to do this. Step forward now and move your parish from being good to being truly great!

We as a church can do so much more to announce the reign of God. We Catholics have a true heart for the poor; we love the liturgical flow of the year; we believe in defending the rejected and the forgotten (in fact, bills that come before the U.S. Congress to do that are known as "Catholic bills"); we're big enough to embrace everyone, and do we ever know how to bury the dead! There's just nothing quite like a Catholic funeral!

And yet, so many pastoral staff people in these "good parishes" complain that attendance is dropping among the young, that collections are too low to meet the demands, that it's harder and harder to recruit volunteers, that we have lost our moral voice in the culture, that we're busy arguing over the language of our rituals while the world is marching to war. We're not working at our Core Work: helping people meet Christ. We're distracted by politics, rubrics, or our own fears.

Dreams and Visions provides a road map toward a new horizon, one that is promised to us by Christ, in the Spirit. So let's get busy and become great!

Bill Huebsch
Pine City, Minnesota
March, 2007

Part One

ESSENTIAL
BACKGROUND

CHAPTER 1

Who Does the Planning for Your Parish?

There are many people working in parish leadership these days, and you're probably one of them. People like you are the backbone of the church. You are of good heart and strong faith. The church has never had so many talented, willing, and able leaders! And parish leaders are working today in this new millennium at a unique moment in church history. We're in a period of great, historic restoration of certain ancient practices of the church, many of which had been out of use for centuries.

One of these ancient practices now being renewed and restored is the catechumenate. That term "catechumenate" is one that unfortunately isn't meaningful yet to many Catholics. It is a word of Greek origin and it refers in general to that process through which newcomers to the faith prepare for baptism, confirmation, and Eucharist. Sometimes we refer to it by its liturgical name, the Rite of Christian Initiation of Adults, or RCIA.

However we refer to it, the practices of the catechumenate are very important to the modern church. They are the bedrock forms of catechesis from which the entire church

Others see Christ in us when we echo our faith.

benefits. When we speak about catechesis (another word of Greek origin!) we refer, of course, to the passing on of the faith from one generation to the next, or even among members of the same generation. "Catechesis" means, literally, "to echo the faith" or to allow faith to be evident in one's life, so much so that others see in us what we see in Christ.

"Others see in us what we see in Christ," the love, sacrifice, and joy that are hallmarks of the followers of Jesus. Others can see that in us, and when they do, they too may become followers of Christ. That's catechesis in its truest form.

WHOLE COMMUNITY CATECHESIS

When we speak today about whole community catechesis, we mean that this echoing of the faith, this *catechesis*, is not meant only for children, but also for adults in the church. It's meant for the *whole community*. Really, it's that simple. And the method by which we provide catechesis for adults grows out of the catechumenate we were discussing just now. The practices of the catechumenate provide a powerful and effective way for us to help adults grow in their faith.

The reason we turn to the catechumenate like this is that many of us adult Catholics in today's church, at least in western nations such as the United States, England, Canada, Ireland, and others, have indeed already been baptized. Most of us were actually baptized as infants. But many of us have not had any faith formation, or any religious education, or any catechesis, or any intentional growth in our faith since those childhood religion classes, whether it was called the

Baltimore Catechism, CCD, or religion class.

Because of that, we are somewhat like those people who join the church for the first time, and we are therefore in need of the kind of faith formation the catechumenate offers. The catechumenate has four stages. 1) Newcomers first pass through an initial inquiry and introduction to the faith. 2) When ready, they publicly state their intentions to the church and enter the catechumenate, which is actually stage two of the process. In this stage, they are introduced in more depth to

If you live in a parish without a current RCIA process operating, or if you simply wish to know more about the catechumenate, go to the pastoral planning Web site at **www. PastoralPlanning. com** and click on "catechumenate links." We'll help you find your way to excellent resources.

the doctrine, prayer life, and mission of the church. During stage two, they are provided a sponsor, an already-committed Christian, who walks with them on their journey of faith. 3) When they are ready (there is no pre-determined length of time for stage two) they request baptism and celebrate their initiation into Christ at the Easter Vigil of that year. 4) After Easter, they enter into a period known as mystagogia, during which they reflect on all that has happened and allow it to live more fully in their hearts.

The entire experience is one whose center-point is conversion to Christ and deepening communion with him. The study of doctrine or church customs, or prayer and spirituality, all follows on that. Conversion precedes catechesis.

Today, because of the strong work of Pope John Paul II in this regard, it is widely understood that all of us Catholics need to deepen our communion with Christ. We need to grow in our love of Scripture. We need to share with each other our journeys of faith. And we need some outright instruction in what it means to be fully Catholic. These are basically the same needs being met in the catechumenate each year. But of course, we can't ask all the adults of the church to re-enter the catechumenate. So in whole community catechesis, *we take elements of that catechumenate and implant them in the rest of parish life.* In a nutshell, this is what we mean by whole community catechesis: the process of implanting in parish life the ancient elements of the catechumenate:

✛ retreats,

✛ breaking open the Word,

✛ encounters,

✛ small communities of growing faith,

✛ adult Faith Gatherings,

✛ liturgical experiences,

✛ a strong focus on Triduum and the paschal mystery,

✛ living as households of faith,

✛ and catechists who are formed for life.

The results of doing this are phenomenal! Already-baptized adults grow in their own faith, seeing Christ as the center of their lives and the church as the community of God. The children's program is much stronger because now the parents are also involved. And the whole parish has more volunteers, more money, more good will, and more vibrant liturgies. It's a win-win-win-win situation.

In whole community catechesis, there is formation in faith, conscience, spirituality, morality, and prayer. This is more than mere *information.* Formation like this involves the whole person, beyond the cognitive. It rises out of an encounter with Christ. It leads to conversion of the heart, to a shift in horizons from following rules and avoiding eternal punishment, to active loving, working for justice, and integrating faith into life. Knowing *about* religion is one thing, but encountering Christ and living the resulting faith is

The catechumenate is the "source of inspiration" for all catechesis, according to the **General Directory** (#91). It is also called the "model for all catechesis" (#59) and helps us realize that beyond understanding doctrine, catechesis must also lead adults to proclaim their faith!

another. It is this latter encounter with its resultant change of heart that catechesis today seeks to encourage and promote.

A LOT OF TALK

There has been a lot of talk about this over the past ten years in the church. Countless documents, books, seminars, workshops, and conferences have pointed to this new movement and explained it. The time has come now to actually *plan* for a way to implement it. And such planning falls to the parish community. Even if the local bishop were to mandate lifelong faith formation, the local parish would still have to create the pastoral plan to make it a reality. And the team within that local parish doing this planning most likely includes the pastor, senior pastoral staff, someone named to coordinate all of this, lay volunteers, and lay leaders. Whoever is on this team, they are called to assist in the mission of the Gospel, the mandate of Jesus to "go and teach" and to assist in that mission by helping the parish envision, invent, and implement ways to reach all adults, youth, children, and guests in every corner of parish life.

So, who are you? Are you a lay volunteer leader? A pastor or bishop? A paid parish staff person? On the staff of a parish school? A volunteer minister in the liturgy or education or pastoral care programs of the parish? As you prepare for this work of pastoral planning, it's important to be aware of your own situation. Read these profiles (read them all, even those not about you) and take a few minutes to get in touch with your own thoughts. These are meant to stimulate you to be clear about your own experience and beliefs about your parish.

Are you a parish leader?

In today's Catholic parish, the number of those who are actively engaged with parish life seems to be getting smaller but you're still engaged yourself. You're a parish leader, helping shape parish life by planning programs and managing budgets and facilities. You're on the parish council, or a finance committee, or some other parish leadership group. You were elected or appointed to this role, and you might even feel that you aren't fully prepared to help lead the parish as you're expected to do. You probably attend many meetings, each with its own agenda. It's frustrating for you sometimes because you sense that the people of the parish are rather indifferent to all that the parish offers. They don't seem to care about the need for a steady stream of income, or about the need to update the buildings, or the need to be actively engaged themselves.

And most likely the other members of the committee or council of which you're a part don't prepare for the meetings very well, or don't even attend them all. Like you, they're busy. Maybe they travel for their work, or commute a long distance daily, or have many family demands. As a result, the meetings aren't always terribly effective. And furthermore, your role is simply to *advise* the parish staff, not to make the final decisions, and you sometimes feel that isn't a very essential thing to do—merely advise someone else.

A lot of good things do happen in the parish!

The parish may have a difficult time filling all the leadership posts, and even though you have thought of resigning, you have agreed to stay on and keep plugging away. Good for you!

A lot of good things do happen in the parish, and a lot of people do have their spiritual needs met by the parish every week. So even though the parish isn't perfect, it's pretty darn good and you're glad to be part of it all.

You personally know many households that aren't active in the parish anymore. Who knows why? Maybe their faith just grew cold. Maybe it's a second or even a third marriage and they don't feel very welcome. Maybe they're living together without the benefit of marriage at all and feel that the church condemns them for it. Or maybe they're using a method of birth control that the church doesn't approve, and they just can't reconcile themselves to being active. They probably haven't had any adult faith development since they were in grade school, so they may have a mistaken idea about what the church teaches. Or maybe one of the members of the household isn't Catholic. It can be tough to remain active when your husband or wife isn't. And parishes aren't always very welcoming to non-Catholic spouses.

Most likely some of these "inactive" Catholics are your own family members, your children or siblings. You might actually feel a little hurt that they're not still faithful Catholics. It's close to home for you

And yet, you're a parish leader. You've chosen to stay and make this parish stronger. You've got dreams and visions for your parish. You want the parish to be more welcoming for all these people. You want your parish to somehow become a magnet that attracts them back. You're searching for an effective way to do this, a pastoral plan for the parish that helps people get active again.

From time to time, the pastor or a parish staff person invites you to attend a training day, usually on a Saturday, usually with an outside speaker, and usually sponsored by the diocese or archdiocese in which your parish is located. The event probably runs from 9 AM to 3 PM, so it takes the whole day, and it's at the diocesan center or at a parish somewhere in the diocese. You pick up some new materials and some new ideas, but you leave wondering how on earth you're supposed to take this home and implement it.

Reflection Pause now to think about the people who volunteer as leaders in your parish. How accurate is this profile of them? If you're one of them, how accurate is it of you? What would you add or take away from this profile to make it more accurate?

Are you a volunteer minister?

In today's parish, the number of people being invited to serve in a public ministry of the church is growing every year, and you are one of these people. You're a volunteer worker, called on to provide a specific ministry, which fifty years ago would have been done exclusively by the priests or sisters. So this means you are volunteering your time and giving your talents in liturgy, or youth ministry, or education, or visiting the sick or homebound, or working in ministries for the poor, or the rejected. Or you might be one of the money counters in the parish, or one of the funeral ministers. Or you're working in one of a dozen other parish ministries.

Because you're actively engaged yourself in parish life, you may have a hard time understanding why more people aren't more active. When new volunteers are needed, you sometimes try to recruit them yourself so you know how difficult it can be. People are busy! They have lots of demands on their time, and more often than not, the parish is a somewhat low priority for them.

But every once in a while someone new shows up, with good energy and lots of talent, so the ranks of the volunteers in your ministry are re-energized and refreshed. Thank goodness for that!

It might even be possible in your parish that the group of volunteers working in music ministry, for example, or in religious education, or on the school fund-raising committee is basically the same as it's been for many years. You might even have inadvertently formed a sort of clique that newcomers find hard to penetrate. New people might feel inhibited to suggest new ideas for fear they'll be told that, in this parish, it has been tried before and failed, so new ideas aren't welcome anymore.

It's great to have you volunteering your time, and since no one else seems to step forward, the parish really needs you to continue.

And yet, new ideas might sometimes help. Like the parish leaders described above, you can also see that fewer people seem active in the parish these days. You would like to attract more people to get involved, but it's a catch-22. In order to make room for new folks, you have to step aside a little. But you have a certain way of doing things and you can't really step aside until someone else learns that, but new people might want to do things differently, so change comes very slowly or not at all.

Every once in a while, the staff person who manages the ministry in which you're involved, be it a lay worker, a sister, or the pastor, asks you to attend a training day somewhere in the diocese or archdiocese. Or maybe the training is being offered right there at your own parish. In either case, this means giving more time to the parish, and time is something you might not have a lot of right now.

But still, father or sister or the lay staff person has told you how important it is to attend these continuing education days, and you are interested in the topic. Many of the other volunteers can't attend for one reason or another, so you do go. The room gradually fills up with volunteers, parish staff people, and a handful of pastors, all from other parishes. The diocesan or archdiocesan staff is also there. A couple of publishers may have display tables set up, probably because they put up the money to bring in the speaker or pay for the lunch.

Finally, the event gets underway. There's a rather long morning prayer, followed by some announcements, and then the speaker is introduced. He's written a couple of books about the topic being addressed, and he's got a PowerPoint presentation running and a flip chart ready to go. You might think to yourself, "If this person's not very good, I'm leaving at noon." A lot of people are actually thinking the same thing.

The first thing this speaker does is to ask a question of the group. "What do you want the outcome of all your efforts to be in your parish? What do you want people to take away from their encounter with the parish? *What do you want to happen as a result of your ministry?*" The whole

> *What do you want to see happen in your parish?*

group sitting in that hall is silent. It's a tough question. So the speaker, who has a sense of humor, says, "This isn't a rhetorical question. I'm expecting someone to answer me." A little laughter and the group is relaxing a little. Bit by bit, the speaker teases out of the group, including you, what outcomes you hope for in your ministry and writes them on that flip chart:

1. More people to be active
2. People to *want* to learn about faith
3. More participation in the liturgy for the parish
4. People to know Christ
5. Parishioners to actually live their faith
6. Parents to get involved with their kids' faith
7. More volunteers
8. And so forth

As you sit there, you really hope this speaker can help you do this. Because, yes, this is exactly what your own dreams and visions for the parish are. It actually helps to hear that people from all these other parishes have the same dreams and visions too. What is the pastoral plan that can deliver this? And how can you take it home to your own parish and implement it? That's the thousand-dollar question, isn't it?

Reflection Pause now to think about the people who volunteer as ministry workers in your parish. How accurate is this profile of them? If you're one of them, how accurate is it of you? What would you add or take away from this profile to make it more accurate?

Are you the pastor?

The last ten years have not been an easy time to be the pastor of a Catholic parish. But here you are, Father. For better or worse, you're the one in charge. You're probably working too hard. Many weeks end up being longer than you planned, even if you have a day off scheduled. A funeral is a funeral, after all. They certainly can't be scheduled very far in advance. And since most of the work you do is behind the scenes, with the sick or dying or during the week days when most parishioners can't see what's happening in the parish, there are most likely some people who think you're not working hard enough!

And for another thing, you simply can't please everybody. Some parishioners are demanding more pious devotional opportunities. Others want more work for social justice. Some want both. A third group just seems to disagree with many church teachings and is angry if you even mention the place of women in the church, or the demand from the chancery to implement the General Instruction of the Roman Missal, or the fact that the parish hasn't bought a new hymnal in almost twenty years. So you tread lightly, not wanting to offend anyone, trying to keep everyone happy.

But it's not easy. You stand in the middle and often take hits from everyone. What you want is not very complicated:

you want people to be active and involved, to sing at Sunday Mass, to increase their contributions a little, to support the building fund, to get along during parish meetings, to even be there to attend those meetings in the first place, and to love the church.

And you also want to make a lasting contribution to this parish. You know that eventually you'll be transferred, but it is important that the pastoral life of this parish be strong. You want to leave it in good shape, and you really want to make a contribution to the lives of the folks here in this parish. So you're seeking a pastoral plan to help you do that.

You may be the pastor of a small, rural parish, or a cluster of parishes. Increasingly, pastors are being called on to serve more than one community. Or maybe you serve an inner-city parish, where funds are tight and the building needs work. More and more men are serving as pastors of multicultural parishes, learning new languages and customs and balancing competing demands. Or you may be pastor of one of those large, suburban parishes with more staff than the diocesan center. Wherever you serve, you share with your brother priests a strong dedication and faith, and great hope for renewal in your parish.

What keeps you up nights is that you know full well that sixty or seventy percent of parents are simply not involved in their kids' religious education. It isn't so much that they're of poor heart or bad intent (most of them want to be good parents, after all) but the church has been providing only children's programs for so long that there just isn't any way for these parents to be part of it. The only exception is first reconciliation and first Eucharist preparation; they are part of that. And what you see then is how really disoriented most of them are about everything having to do with the church.

What are your dreams and visions for the parish you pastor?

And if you confirm in junior or senior years of school, you know that once they've got the sacrament, that crowd of young people is going to disappear. As their pastor, you hope they'll come back one day, but you feel almost powerless to hang on to them now.

You know that it's tough to reach out to the divorced and remarried, a large number in your parish. And yet, you know also that those first marriages were often entered into when they were just kids—too young really—and now here they are, finally married to someone wonderful for them, living in a real "holy bond" but, of course, it's a marriage which the church doesn't bless. You're inclined to defend the new and real bonds of marriage in which they're now living, but you also know you can't.

Then there are those others who are living outside the norm of the church. You want to welcome them without appearing to break the rules. You know that people are inactive for a reason, be it their disagreement with the church, or a lack of an initial encounter with Christ, or the result of a mixed marriage, or that they simply wandered away slowly and now don't have a clue how to return. And after people have been away from actively practicing their faith for a while, it's tough to find an avenue back. At the moment the pastoral plan for these inactive ones is that they're supposed to pick up their phone and call you as pastor to make an appointment to go to confession. Technically, they're living in sin. The way back is to confess and get absolution, a long-standing pastoral practice of the church.

But you know most people aren't going to do that. In fact, they might be inactive in part *because* of confession. A lot of people fear this sacrament and not very many people participate in it, including the active Catholics. So as a pastoral plan, you are very aware that this simply isn't enough.

This situation: so many inactive people with no real plan to get them re-engaged with their faith; this is what keeps you up at night. Your own dreams and visions for the parish have to do with helping these folks find an avenue home.

Every now and then, someone on the bishop's staff sends out a notice about a training day for liturgists or catechists or even for the whole parish staff. If you have the day free and no funeral comes up, you can attend. But quite honestly, what's going to change if you do attend and listen to some speaker explain a new approach to this or that? You've been down that road before and tried everything.

There's been a lot of talk in recent years about the need for lifelong formation for people, about the need to offer adults some form of religious education or formation. They call it "whole community catechesis" or something similar to that, but, even though the ideas are good ones, and some of the plans seem doable, it's the adults themselves who don't seem to care. How do you get people to take part in something that they just don't seem interested in? The best ideas in the world don't help if people aren't interested.

And what really hurts and bothers you is that some families who were formerly in your parish have actually found a home in another denomination. They were invited by a neighbor or friend or co-worker to start attending the Glory of God Community Church around the corner and now they go there every week, contributing time and money to this more evangelical community. Why? What is that church offering to them that you aren't? It isn't so much that you feel competitive with this other denomination, but that you know we Catholics have a major contribution to make in people's lives, and it frustrates you when someone in the parish simply goes elsewhere.

So back to what we said earlier. As pastor, you really do want to help people grow in their faith. You want to help them become more active in parish life. You want them to know Christ and love the church. But what's the pastoral plan to help you do this? You need a new approach, but it has to really work this time.

Reflection Pause now to think about the pastor (or pastoral coordinator if there is no priest in your parish). How accurate is this profile? If you're one of them, how accurate is it of you? What would you add or take away from this profile to make it more accurate?

Are you a parish staff person?

The day-to-day work of our Catholic parishes is increasingly being put into the hands of lay or religious men and women. We call them "the parish staff." And if you're one of them, you probably have done some advanced study of theology and are well prepared for the work you do. Your commitment is clear because you work long hours at a rather low wage, but you aren't doing it for the money in the first place. You're in this ministry because you believe that the church needs you, and that the people around you need a strong, effective parish community.

Like the others, you struggle to keep people engaged. And for you, this is very personal. This is your job, after all. This is what you've dedicated your life to, and you want others to be just as committed as you are. Like the pastor (and maybe you're acting as the pastor, depending on the parish) you're so busy in the midst of weekly ministry needs that it's hard to see the bigger picture. It's hard to look beyond your own very busy ministry to consider a larger pastoral plan that would engage the whole parish.

And, even though you don't intend for this to happen, you do have to spend a little time and energy defending your own turf in the parish. After all, you do have a ministry area for which you're responsible, be it liturgy or religious education or pastoral care or administration. You can't just let go of this and assume someone else will get things done. And you have your core group of volunteers, which you have carefully cultivated and trained, and you don't want to do anything to upset them or make them think they aren't needed.

You may work on a larger staff of professional ministers, each of whom is somewhat isolated from the others, in somewhat "watertight silos." Each ministry area has its own budget, its own goals, and its own constituency within the parish. Bridging these areas isn't easy. It takes lots of time and new thinking. There is so much work to do, and so many deadlines as each liturgical year, or school year, unfolds, that shifting gears and moving in some new direction seems pretty impractical.

You get a lot of mail from the diocesan or archdiocesan pastoral center, not to mention from a host of Catholic publishers. You're often invited to attend this or that day of enrichment, or formation, or training, or whatever. From time to time, you do take part in these days, but you return home to your parish office, look through the mail, answer a few phone calls, and get ready for the event that evening— and to be honest, from year to year, not that much changes, despite what the guest speaker had to say. It's great to consider new ideas, but in the end, someone has to get the work done. You can't just let it all go and focus on every new idea that comes along.

But gnawing at the back of your mind is the reality in the church today that many people really do not believe the church loves them and supports them. They take only a minimal part in parish life, getting their kids into religious ed or through the sacraments, but not feeling deeply committed—and also not giving much time or money to parish needs. You know these people, better maybe than anyone, because you see them when they have needs. You're gracious with them, welcoming, inviting, but for some reason they remain at the edge of parish life. Your own dreams and visions for the parish have to do with helping get such people re-engaged. But how?

Reflection Pause now to think about the people who work as the staff in your parish. How accurate is this profile of them? If you're one of them, how accurate is it of you? What would you add or take away from this profile to make it more accurate?

SO, WHAT'S THE PLAN?

These four groups of people—lay leaders, volunteer ministers, pastors, and parish staff people—they are the core planners for any parish. Each comes to planning with his or her own presumptions, experiences, expectations, and beliefs. Ever since the close of Vatican II nearly fifty years ago, Catholic parishes have been organizing themselves in the way they do now. What would it take to improve on that?

CHAPTER 2

What Do Church Leaders Want You to Do?

A lot has been happening in the universal Catholic Church over the past fifty years regarding the pastoral plan of the parish. Pastoral planning is the sort of ministry that evolves from the direction for the parish that is set by the leaders. One doesn't begin by planning. One begins by studying the course that the church is taking and shaping a plan to follow that course.

So what is this new course? As a leader, volunteer worker, pastor, or pastoral staff person, how do you know what direction the leaders of the church want you to follow?

One way to know this is to turn to the papal and other universal or international Catholic meetings, documents, and statements. Another is to look at what the bishops of any given nation have set down as a direction for that particular church. And a third is to look at the activities and developments of the faithful who are working in universities, diocesan offices, and parishes.

We're going to do that here in a quick survey of all that's been happening in the years since 1960. But first, let's turn to "the back of the book" and look at the ending. What

A powerful reform is underway in catechesis and evangelization.

you'll find is that these have been the most dynamic and exciting years of renewal in the church since the early centuries of the church's founding. There has been enormous activity surrounding catechesis and liturgy— study weeks, synods of bishops, papal documents, conferences of bishops' statements, a major new catechism, the restoration of the catechumenate, renewal movements, youth ministry development, more papal documents, more study, whole university programs created to study all of this, and conference after conference after conference. We've seen nothing like this in the church in all of its history!

The new sense of direction which is emerging from all this has the power to really effectively announce the Reign of God, to provide a true spiritual home for people of all nations, and to chart the course for justice and peace that is the dream of the Gospels. Pope John Paul II often spoke of a new evangelization, but there's also a new catechesis emerging. Taken together and implemented in any given parish, this is a more powerful reform on the local level than anything that happened during the course of Vatican II itself, except for the reform of the sacraments and liturgies of the church.

Indeed, as you will see here, the strong work of the past five or six decades provides a clear sense of direction for the church. But we all have to be ready to embrace the change in parish structure needed to bring this about. Whatever role you play, whether you're the bishop or diocesan staff person overseeing your whole diocese, or a parish worker focused more directly on one community of that diocese, the work of implementing this bold new sense of direction, this bold new pastoral plan, falls now to you.

THE 1960S

On the eve of the Second Vatican Council, the pastoral plan of the church seemed quite simple. Bishops and pastors provided all the leadership, while sisters and brothers handled the education and health care systems of the church. Lay people attended Mass weekly, followed the moral and devotional direction set for them by the leaders, and used the sacrament of confession to reconcile themselves if they went astray.

Catechesis was based solely on the *Roman Catechism* from 1566 where answers to specific questions of faith and doctrine were memorized, along with prayers, lists, and other details of Catholic life. By and large in the United States, Canada, England, Wales, and Ireland, Catholics lived what was known as a "Catholic life." Everyday life was imbued with Catholic customs, beliefs, and traditions. So much was this the case that "catechism class" (as it was known in some parts of the church) had only a very small gap to fill. The actual instruction was done through all the other means: home life, devotions, traditions, personal piety, fasting, abstinence, and obedience to church norms, and of course, weekly confession and Mass attendance.

The pastoral plan for parishes had remained essentially the same since the sixteenth century. There had been so little change, in fact, during those four or five hundred years between Trent and Vatican II that when the bishops and theologians at Vatican II did begin to reform the church, it came as quite a shock to many people. Having been held in

For more resources on Vatican II, including access to **Vatican II in Plain English**, visit the pastoral planning Web site at **www.PastoralPlanning.com** and click on "Vatican II."

place so long by the sheer force of the discipline of the church's leaders and the threat of hell, that old "Catholic life" now began to unravel and the need for a more vigorous catechesis became strong.

Here was Vatican II calling for "full, active and conscious participation in the liturgy." Catechesis would be needed. The Council was calling for lay people to engage the world and contribute to it from their faith, to animate that world with the Spirit of Christ. Catechesis would be needed. Vatican II spoke about a universal call to holiness. Catechesis would be needed. Vatican II led us toward charitable and prayerful ecumenical and interfaith relationships and dialogue. Catechesis would be needed. Vatican II described conscience as the place where we are alone with God, whose voice echoes in our depths. Catechesis would be needed. Vatican II restored the catechumenate, which had not been active in the church for nearly seventeen hundred years. Catechesis would be needed. Vatican II restored our understanding of baptism as the essential sacerdotal sacrament. Catechesis would be needed.

But in fact, the church did not have a tradition of catechesis then. It had only catechisms to memorize. Memorization is certainly part of any form of learning, but no one would seriously argue that it is sufficient to have mere cognitive recognition of doctrine and tradition. The memorization of those years, however, as we said above, fit into a whole

Catholic life that was distinguished from every other religion on earth. The actual formation in faith happened not in catechism class but in daily life.

Today we understand that there must also be a strong element of the emotive and intuitive in faith formation. The heart must be committed to Christ if one's faith is to be strong. We do not, after all, place our faith in the church itself. The church is not God. It's not enough to merely know *about* one's faith or church. Knowing about the church doesn't make you Christian. For example, it's possible to study Judaism thoroughly: the prayers, prophets, history, traditions, rituals, people—all of it. That would not make you a Jew. So it is with Christianity. What makes us Christian is an encounter with the risen Christ, God's own Son, revealing God's own heart to us.

At Vatican II, not much debate about catechesis was held. It was generally agreed at that time that we did not do very adequate catechesis within the church. In fact, the catechumenate itself had fallen out of use, almost entirely. In the history of the church, one struggles to find meaningful references to catechumenal practice after the fourth century or so. And with the advent of modern times, the church addressed mainly the catechetical needs of children after baptism. It centered this catechetical work on preparation for the sacraments, which in time came to act almost like graduation. Once a person had been confirmed, he or she was finished with faith formation. Indeed, parishes helped create this thinking by offering almost no formal faith formation for anyone older than high school age.

The church had long hoped to engage all adults in the catechetical process. And in fact, we have come to realize now that the primary aim of such catechesis in the church is conversion, not instruction. But Vatican II itself, as it turned out, would not be the moment in our history where the needed development of catechesis would happen. In fact, at the council, the only direct reference to catechesis comes in article forty-four of the "Decree on the Pastoral Office of Bishops in the Church." There it calls for a series of "general directories" to be drawn up after the council. These were to address, for example, the care of souls, the pastoral care of special groups, "and also a directory for the catechetical instruction of the Christian people in which the fundamental principles of this instruction and its organization will be dealt with…"

The Council Fathers were aware that already afoot throughout the world was a catechetical renewal. The search was already underway "for a better method than the questions and answers of the catechism," as Sr. Kate Dooley pointed out in an essay published in *The Echo Within* (Notre Dame: Ave Maria Press, 1997). In the early 1900s, catechetical leaders meeting in southern Germany were testing new methods. They recognized that merely knowing facts about the faith was not the same as encountering Christ and hearing the Gospel proclaimed!

The so-called "kerygmatic movement" of the 1950s went even further, moving us "to recapture the spirit and vision of the church of the apostolic and patristic era" (Dooley). This movement added the element of "formation" to the memorized catechism. Learners received the proclamation of the Gospel, the teachings of Jesus, and the saving acts of his life, death, and resurrection.

This movement was based on "four signs" that were to be in balance for a proper understanding of the faith:

✙ Liturgy

✙ Scripture

✙ Church teaching

✙ The witness of Christian living.

"Catechesis was no longer limited to instruction and to the classroom" (Dooley). Instead, it merged with liturgy, biblical study, and discipleship into an organic whole, just as it was experienced in the early church. We are grateful to Josef Jungmann, SJ (1889-1975), who taught pastoral theology on the faculty of the University of Innsbruck, for these insights, which are becoming part and parcel of all effective catechesis today.

In the United States, Jungmann's work was popularized by Jesuit and religion educator Johannes Hofinger (1905-1984). It was mainly by Hofinger's efforts that a series of international catechetical study weeks were held in

✙ Niejmegen, 1959

✙ Eichstatt, 1960

✙ Bangkok, 1962

✙ Katigondo, 1964

✙ Manila, 1967

✙ Medellin, 1968.

These study weeks, as you can see, anticipated Vatican II and continued during and after it. They had influence on the council itself. The Eichstatt week had particular influence as it laid out principles of liturgical and catechetical renewal. But it was at Medellin, Columbia, in 1968 that serious reflection on evangelization led to a new focus. It was seen during the week in Medellin that we cannot presuppose faith in members of the church. Baptism is no guarantee that people have come to encounter Christ and adhere to him and the church with their whole hearts. It does not guarantee deep communion with Christ.

The work at Medellin was landmark, and it came to be the turning point in our fuller understanding of catechesis. It summarized all the previous study weeks and led to the renewal that we now have in the church.

Following Medellin, Pope Paul VI published the *General Catechetical Directory* (GCD) in 1971, which provided a framework on which a great deal of catechetical renewal was built. This directory reflected all the work done to that point at the various study weeks and at the council. But the document contained a few lines in paragraph twenty which may have gone largely unnoticed by many. These lines, it turns out, helped set the stage for much that would follow:

> [Bishops] should remember that catechesis for adults, since it deals with persons who are capable of an adherence that is fully responsible, must be considered the chief form of catechesis. All other forms, which are indeed always necessary, are in some way oriented to it.

The GCD was enculturated in the United States by way of a "Pastoral Message on Catholic Education" issued by the U.S. Catholic bishops in 1972, called *To Teach as Jesus Did*, which provided impetus for much growth in catechesis in this country. In this document, the bishops said, in article 43, "Today it is important to recognize that learning is a lifelong experience." The bishops were setting the stage for a new pastoral plan for the church, one that includes more than children's religious education. They went on in this document to call for balance among all the elements of catechetical need within the parish: adults, youth, schools, children, and others.

A principle architect of the bishops' message was Bishop Raymond Lucker who was the main force behind it and the organizer of the effort to produce it. It is possible that no bishop in the U.S. church had given as much careful thought to catechesis as Lucker. Raised in both urban and rural settings in Minnesota, he was ordained in 1952 and assigned as assistant director in the Archdiocese of St. Paul for the Confraternity of Christian Doctrine (CCD) office. He earned two doctorates, one in education at the University of Minnesota and one in theology in Rome. In his doctoral thesis for this latter degree (which was published as a book) Lucker gives a long, detailed history of catechesis, and he notes that after the reformation, catechesis became concerned with:

> knowledge of what we must believe to get to heaven. And for the next four hundred years one of the most important aims of religious education will be to equip the child to defend his faith against the attacks of the heretics and to answer their objections. (*The Aims of Religious Education, in the Early Church and in the American Catechetical Movement.* Rome, Italy: Catholic Book Publishing Co., 1966, p. 110)

The fundamental aims of teaching religion, however, he argued in this same doctoral thesis, must be:

> to develop a living, personal faith, to bring the students to a complete conversion of life, to inspire commitment to Christ, and to help them enter into communion with God. The writer of this paper is in full accord with these aims. (p. 222)

Lucker later served as director of the Department of Education at the United States Catholic Conference,

> *The greatest need
> in the church
> [is for] an
> educated laity.*
>
> — BISHOP O'HARA

in Washington, DC. He was ordained an auxiliary bishop of the Archdiocese of St. Paul and Minneapolis in 1971 and later served for twenty-five years (to the day) as bishop of the Diocese of New Ulm in Minnesota, where his own conversion to Christ played a central role in his extensive public teaching. He died of a melanoma on September 19, 2001.

Earlier in his life, Lucker had fallen under the influence of Archbishop Edwin O'Hara who believed that the plan to have every child in a Catholic school did not serve the church as well as some thought it would. Instead, O'Hara felt that "the greatest need in the church was [for] an educated laity, people who were committed to their faith and were interested in handing it on to others" (Lucker in November 1994, in an address which was part of the St. Paul Seminary Centennial Lecture series. The paper he gave is archived at the University of St. Thomas. I take these notes from the paper written by William McDonough which is cited in the acknowledgments.).

In 1964, Lucker co-wrote an essay with Theodore Stone in which they expressed strong belief in what was emerging as the new catechesis.

> [The historical development in catechesis] might give the impression that first comes instruction, then formation, and finally the personal meeting between God and the student. The reverse however is more correct. Communion with God ordinarily does not take place at the end of the religion lesson, but rather

whenever God approaches through sacred signs (biblical, liturgical, witness, or doctrinal signs)…to transform one's mentality. ("Formation and Training of Lay Catechists" in *Pastoral Catechetics.* New York: Herder and Herder, 1964, p. 239)

Bishops from other nations such as England, Wales, and Canada also began laying the groundwork for an approach to catechesis that addressed more than children. Indeed, if we are to be successful with the children in the first place, we know that their parents must be involved at every level of faith formation. Without the parents, all our efforts amount to "seed falling on rocky ground." Faith will sprout because of our efforts, but the real harvest of faith can only be sustained within the home.

In 1974, an international synod of bishops dealt in great depth with the question of evangelization raised at Medellin, but they did not publish any outcomes. Instead, they encouraged Pope Paul VI to reflect on their findings, which he did, publishing an apostolic exhortation in 1975, *Evangelii Nuntiandi* or, in English, "On Evangelization in the Modern World." It was received with tremendous grace by the church. At the time, it was arguably the most important document issued in the church since the close of Vatican II. It is concise (only five chapters long), vibrant, readable, and profound. In article four, the pope posed his leading question: "At this turning point of history, does the church or does she not find herself better equipped to proclaim the Gospel and to put it into people's hearts with conviction, freedom of spirit, and effectiveness?"

Notice this question. It is a thoroughly modern concern, rooted in today's situation. It is challenging. It is Christ-centered and focused on the Gospel, the kerygma. And it is powerful: Do we have conviction? Is there freedom of spirit? And, mainly, are we *effective*? And most important, this document marked a turning point for pastoral planners. Whereas in the past, the concern was for Catholics to be thoroughly familiar with the church, its teachings, laws, liturgies, and traditions, now it seems the concern shifts to something more Christ-centered. As a Catholic, do you know Christ? Have you experienced the life-changing power of an initial encounter with Christ? In other words, have you been "converted?" Conversion to Christ of this sort, the *General Directory for Catechesis* would later argue, *precedes* catechesis (article 62).

This key turning point has led, of course, to decades of work on what we call "evangelization." For Catholics, this is a difficult term and yet another word with Greek origins. Catholics don't know much about conversion to Christ. It sounds vaguely "protestant" to us. And yet, if you examine the message of Pope John Paul II, the first pope in the church after this document was promulgated, you'll find him to be profoundly Christ-centered. Everywhere he went in the world—at clergy gatherings, in meetings of men and women religious, in preparation for the Jubilee Year, at academic meetings, youth rallies, or masses for the throngs—his message was similar. "Come to Christ. Do not be afraid. Give your heart to Christ. Open wide the doors to Christ."

He saw Christ as the Lord of the universe and the center of all humankind. It was fundamental to him. It was an insight that he himself gained through the Spirit.

In 1977, a second international synod of bishops met in Rome with catechesis as its focus, no doubt preparing to draw up that directory which had been called for in article forty-four of the document on bishops at the Council.

Bishop Raymond Lucker attended this synod as one of four official delegates from the U.S. Conference of Bishops. While at the synod, Lucker gave a speech to the assembled bishops in which he said:

> [T]he most pressing need in the church is the evangelization and catechesis of adults [as] the *General Catechetical Directory* so forcibly reminded us....We have neglected the central goal of catechesis which is to strengthen faith. And we have almost totally ignored the evangelization of the Catholic people....I say that the key to the catechesis of children and youth is the catechesis of adults. ("Needed: Adult Catechesis." *Origins* 7/18. October 20, 1977, 276-277)

But Lucker also was about to make a key point which we now embrace as a vital step in successful catechesis for the whole community. In this same speech at the synod, he said:

> First...people come to an initial faith. They accept Jesus as Lord...and in a general way respond....We call this evangelization. Then comes catechesis, which presupposes this initial faith and is concerned with nurturing it, strengthening it, and making it mature.

Reflection When you read Bishop Lucker's comments above, what strikes you most strongly about them? How do you connect them to the pastoral planning needs of your parish?

As the synod ended, the bishops issued a message to the people of God regarding their findings, and they also sent a set of resolutions to Pope Paul VI. Two years later, in 1979, Paul John Paul II issued the apostolic exhortation, *Catechesi*

For more information about the General Directory, including access to **The General Directory for Catechesis in Plain English,** visit the pastoral planning Web site at **www.PastoralPlanning.com** and click on "GDC."

Tradendae, or in English, "On Catechesis in Our Time."

This exhortation laid the groundwork for a high-level renewal of catechesis in today's church. It begins by reiterating what Paul VI had said earlier, catechesis is Christ-centered and it is rooted in tradition. Evangelization is the overarching activity, and catechesis is one dimension of that. The main sources, as directed by Vatican II's *Dogmatic Constitution on Divine Revelation,* are Scripture and tradition. It also treats various practical aspects of catechesis and concludes by saying, in essence, that catechesis isn't just for children; *it's for everyone.*

And of course, once again, this document proclaimed that the definitive aim of catechesis is "to put people not only in touch but in communion, in intimacy, with Jesus Christ," as Bishop Lucker had forcefully argued. Later in his own diocese, Bishop Lucker instructed his people in these words:

> Every parish…needs opportunities for adults to come together to pray, to witness to God's gifts in their lives, and to grow in the knowledge and love of Jesus.…If this means that classroom instruction has to be suspended for a time while the teachers are being formed, so be it. Nothing can replace adult growth in faith. (*Prairie Views: Twenty-Five Years of Pastoral Letters*)

Then in 1997, with the approval of Pope John Paul II, the *General Directory for Catechesis* was published. Drawing on the wisdom and spirit of all the work mentioned above, and much that is not mentioned here for the sake of brevity, the GDC provides sound, workable principles on which we can base our current work in catechesis.

Whole community catechesis arises from the GDC. The name itself, "whole community" comes from article 254 where it says:

"The whole Christian community is the origin, locus, and goal of catechesis. Proclamation of the Gospel always begins with the Christian community and invites [people] to conversion and the following of Christ."

The U.S. Catholic bishops have taken up both the spirit and the letter of the international and papal documents with great fervor. Writing in 1999 in "Our Hearts Were Burning Within Us," the bishops said this:

We, as the Catholic bishops of the United States, call the church in our country to a renewed commitment to adult faith formation, positioning it at the heart of our catechetical vision and practice. We pledge to support adult faith formation without weakening our commitment to our other essential educational ministries. This pastoral plan guides the implement-ation of this pledge and commitment. (#6)

The U.S. bishops join other conferences of bishops around the world in calling for adult catechesis to be the new norm in parish life. The church—leaders, workers, people—is seeking a way for parishes to bring adults into the circle of

For electronic access to many of the documents discussed in this chapter, visit the pastoral planning Web site at **www.PastoralPlanning.com** and click on "documents." You will also find access on this site to various documents that you can obtain for your library, by clicking on "library."

catechesis within each parish. We want to provide formation for the *whole community*. It is not a shift *away* from children. It is a shift to a wider circle, a more inclusive method, which adults as well as children will appreciate.

And this, in turn, leads us to a new urgency for pastoral planning. What plan can we undertake that will deliver these goals? How will we at once sustain and improve children's catechesis while also providing intense, systematic, and comprehensive catechesis for people of all ages within the parish?

Before we turn to that all-important work of pastoral planning, there is one more urgent question. If Bishop Lucker is correct, *conversion to Christ precedes catechesis.* In 1986, when the U.S. bishops met at St. John's Abbey and University in Collegeville, Minnesota, Lucker addressed them on the vocation of the laity, and he said explicitly, "In my opinion, the most serious problem facing the church is the need for conversion among adult Catholics" ("Linking Church and World: Vocations of the Laity," *Origins* 16. July 3, 1986: 146-152).

Reflection Thinking back over what we just covered in this chapter, what strikes you most strongly? What do you hear that is most profound?

Let's take some time to consider what we mean by conversion, and how it can become a dimension of pastoral planning in the church.

CHAPTER 3

What Exactly Is Conversion?

FIRST, A STORY...

I used to know this fellow, an older gentleman, who was a lifelong Catholic. He went to Mass every week and sometimes more often. He contributed money to his parish faithfully and was active in supporting parish needs. He sent his kids to religious education at the parish, and he and his wife developed a home in which prayer was common, in which the annual procession of Catholic feasts was evident, and in which the poor were cared for generously. Every evening, this fellow knelt down beside his bed to say his evening prayers. He was, indeed, a "good Catholic."

But when he was in his seventies, his wife, who had been ill with the disease for seven years, died of Alzheimer's. In his typically generous and caring way, he had nursed his wife through thick and thin with the disease, until he could no longer handle her alone. For a while, someone lived in with them to help provide care, but finally and reluctantly, a nursing home was necessary. Even there, he visited faithfully while she was in apparent oblivion about who he was.

The saddest aspect of her dying years was the loss of their shared dreams for retirement. They had worked their entire lives to support a large family, and now that the kids were grown and on their own, it would have been their chance to enjoy each other and travel, cook together, garden, or simply sit quietly in the house, reading in the evening. The powerful presence of one's most beloved companion, however, was lost to the disease. He lost her. She slipped away slowly and painfully while he watched. The sadness was overwhelming for everyone.

And then she was dead. The aloneness which creeps in when a beloved spouse is declining was now palpable. The loss of physical affection, a touch, a look, a smile or laugh— now loomed larger than life itself. At least, while she was sick, she was present in some form, even if unrecognizable. But now even that was lost.

So Herb was alone. He gradually did allow his life to return to a normal state—daily meals, Sunday Mass, visits from the grandkids, the garden in spring, the newspaper, a few favorite TV shows. But of course, an abiding sense of loss and the permanency of his wife's death remained with him.

Then one day, his neighbor George dropped by for the visit that changed his life forever. George invited and convinced Herb to attend a three-day weekend retreat, a Cursillo. Off he went, having no idea what to expect.

When he returned home, Herb's family wasn't sure what to do with him! There was a new light in his eye, a new sense of purpose, a strong and powerful new happiness. He also wanted to hug them all! Hugging wasn't really part of this family's culture. But he'd been hugging fellow retreatants all weekend long. The embraces were part of the Christian culture of love, offering one another support and affection in Christ. Herb was truly touched by it all—and to be honest, since his wife had been ill, he hadn't had much true affection in his life for a while.

Herb also returned home with his own Bible. To his grown children, this seemed odd indeed, and they wondered if he was really still a Catholic. They'd always owned a family Bible, but of course as Catholics they had never read it. But now here was their dad, with his own Bible. He'd written his name inside the cover, and had underlined and highlighted certain favorite verses. The book itself was soon stuffed with prayer cards and book marks.

Herb returned home, too, with a strong love for the Eucharist. During the Cursillo, the group had celebrated the Eucharist twice and each time was very powerful. He'd been attending Mass every week for seventy-two years, but now in this moment of conversion, the Mass seemed like so much more! It was clearer to him now that this powerful celebration was the center point of his Christian faith.

He returned home with a strong and new love for the rejected and poor, for the ones closest to Jesus' own heart. At the Cursillo, he had read Matthew, chapter 25, as if for the first time. In fact, it may well have been the first time. He heard the Scriptures proclaimed at Mass, of course, but those readings did not sink into his consciousness as it did when he read and meditated on the Word himself and shared it with others. With a great force, he began to understand that following Christ means loving the poor.

But the most important change had to do with Herb's general view of life. He had turned from a time of great sadness to one of absolute radiance. He had back that old twinkle in his eye, a quick laugh, a ready affirmation of all he saw that was good—and he saw plenty now! He had shifted from the darkness and loneliness of death to the light and joy of what could only be described as "new life."

These changes were profound and powerful for Herb and, because Cursillo offered follow-up gatherings with others who made the retreat, they were sustained in Herb's life and gradually shifted his entire horizon of faith. When he finally died many years later, this initial encounter, which led him to deep communion with God, proved to have been a major turning point in his life.

What Herb experienced is what we want for every adult in the church!

A few weeks after Herb returned home from the retreat, he was out fishing with one of his sons one evening. He was no preacher, no "evangelist." But as his son pressed him to share a little more about what happened to him at the retreat and its obvious results in his life, Herb found himself telling his son something like this: "All my life I had faith in the church. I believed that if I did what the church told me to, that someday I'd be with mom in heaven. But now I understand that my faith has to be in Christ, in the Lord. It's knowing Christ that leads me to the church."

But what went on during this retreat to make this change happen? his son wondered. So Herb told him. During the retreat, he said, there was a talk on something sort of new to him, called "the paschal mystery." This talk focused on what it means to die in Christ, to enter into the death of the Lord as we do in baptism. Herb's son was truly amazed that his seventy-two year old dad was able to speak with such clarity about this, using such new language. Talking like this had never been part of Herb's family culture.

He went on, explaining to his son: there was a talk on "what it means to die in Christ" by a very good presenter, then my small group had a discussion about it together, and we were each asked to reflect on how we were ourselves entering into the death of the Lord *in our own lives*. I'd honestly never considered this before. But as we talked, slowly it began to dawn on me that caring for mom the way I did all those years, losing her, going through that death, was how I was personally called to "die in Christ." It all made sense. It gave new meaning to everything for me. I'm not alone. If I turn my heart to Christ, and share that with others, then I come out on the other side of all this with hope and even with happiness. It's a whole new experience for me. I still go fishing. I still work in my garden. I'm the same guy," he told his son, "but there's a new light in it all for me. I have a stronger sense of God's presence every day. I know there is purpose, direction, and meaning."

Well, it would be an understatement to say that his son was stunned by this speech. He had never in all his life heard his dad talking like this.

Reflection Do you know someone (maybe yourself) who has experienced this initial encounter with Christ, leading to deeper communion with God? Spend some time in the next month or so listening to the stories from such folks. Let it sink into your own consciousness how vitally important it is for people to begin their journey of faith with such a moment, as St. Paul did on the road to Damascus.

On this retreat, Herb had what we call an "initial encounter with Christ." Even though he'd been baptized many years before and had been a church-going Catholic his entire life, this initial encounter now reshaped everything for him.

And the initial encounter was sustained by the follow-up gatherings of others who'd also had that same experience. Herb had turned his heart to Christ, had turned toward the face of God, and had experienced true conversion.

This is the conversion about which Bishop Lucker was so personally convinced. Those who knew him were aware that he, too, had passed through such an initial conversion, sustained by liturgy, prayer, faith sharing, community meals, and similar experiences.

So what is this? What happens when someone experiences this initial turning of the heart to Christ?

WE CAN'T SEE IT HAPPEN

We can't really see conversion happen, not in the same way that we watch a movie unfold, for example, or watch a ball game progress. Conversion is the work of the Spirit within us. We place ourselves in a position where an opportunity for conversion is possible, and the Spirit does the work.

Normally, the moment of conversion is linked to faith sharing. Somehow in talking about our faith with others, the Spirit touches our own hearts. It is personal, meaning that each of us experiences this at our own time and in our own way. But it is not private. Faith is shared, not hoarded. It is abundant, not scarce. And yet, we cannot really see it until we look back at those moments.

In the catechumenate, there is an ancient practice in the church known as mystagogy. Here we have yet another word with its origins in Greek. It's worth understanding what this word means because it's the avenue to being able to recognize our own conversion. The word itself means something like, "reflecting on mysteries." The practice of mystagogy is to pause after an experience (of any kind; it

*We look into
our lives to
find signs
of conversion to
Christ.*

needn't be overtly religious) recall the experience, and reflect on what touched your heart, what remains in your memory about this experience. Another way into mystagogy is to ask what struck me in this, what did I see or hear—or smell or touch? Mystagogy leads us to be able to see the signs of God's presence, even while we cannot see God.

SIGNS OF CONVERSION

So we look in our lives and the lives of those around us for *signs of conversion.* If we can see signs that the Spirit is moving and shaping us, then conversion is going on.

For example, conversion leads us to a supple sense of self, and we find we are able to adapt to the ebb and flow of life more easily. We come to understand that we need not cling too rigidly to the dock, but we can swim out into daily life with confidence and without fear. This is a sign that conversion is happening within us.

Another sign of conversion is a growing flexibility with others. Just as we can sense ourselves bending with the Spirit, being more supple, so we allow others to have their own experiences, too. We are less judgmental and more accepting. We find that those teachings of Jesus on the Mount are taking hold. Now they are more than mere words of Scripture, but an actual way of life for us: "Do not judge, so that you may not be judged" (Mt 7:1).

A third sign of conversion in our lives is a growing sense of generosity, with money, time, material things, and even with our own inner lives. Many times we begin to operate in life as though everything is scarce and we must gather and hoard in order to have enough. But when we are in Christ, a trust overtakes us that changes that. Again, the teachings of Jesus take on a whole new and real meaning, "Give to everyone who begs from you, and do not refuse anyone who wants to borrow from you" (Mt 5:42).

A fourth sign might be that we grow in patience with others as they sort out their lives. We find ourselves forgiving freely when someone wrongs us. Forgiveness like this frees us more than the other. It allows us to let go and hold no grudge. These others who hurt or disappoint us can often become our "enemies." We hold them at arm's length, keep them at a distance. But when we experience conversion, we find that we are just less focused on all that. A certain grace of forgiveness sweeps in. This is a "given-ness" before the hurt. It's an *unconditional* attitude on our part that, in Christ, the positive energy of love trumps the negative energy of dislike, indifference, or hate. We learn to forgive "seventy times seven times."

Another sign of conversion in our lives is that we find we have a stronger sense of hospitality toward others, strangers as well as friends. We find ourselves living with real day-to-day love for others, affirming them, loving them, and caring for them. This is genuine, not forced. It's a spontaneous expression of love, prompted by the Spirit within.

We develop also a heart for the materially poor. This is no small thing in the Gospels, which are packed with warnings about the dangers of wealth. "Do not store up for yourselves treasures on earth, where moth and rust consume and where thieves break in and steal," we are warned in Matthew 6:19–21. "But store up for yourselves treasures in heaven…for where your treasure is, there your heart will be also."

We become aware of our own failure and sin, and freely realize that we are, indeed, only earthen vessels. We grow into prayerful people. We see the events of daily life through the lens of the Gospel. We have a strong sense of the presence of God. We find a deep, abiding joy. We see ourselves as part of the community of God. We celebrate the sacraments with new energy and life. We sing with full voice. We see in others the very Christ in whom we believe. We get a sense of our own vocation to care for others and lead them to Christ. The list of signs goes on.

A key sign of conversion is a deep love for the Eucharist, not as a private devotion, but as that big, messy shared event we hold on Sunday mornings together. Parishes find that as members have this initial experience of conversion, their liturgies begin to soar. People sing with full hearts, and there is a strong sense of prayerfulness. The community feels united and purposeful. In short, the full, active participation called for at Vatican II comes into reality—as a result of being in a converted parish community.

Likewise it is true that people who are in Christ are just generous with both their money and their talents. People step forward because the Spirit living within them urges them to. They take more risks, are willing to give their time, and they do so with excitement rather than reluctance.

And finally, a sure sign of conversion is a *desire* for more faith formation. Once such an initial encounter is experienced, people want more. They now want to grow in their faith. The doldrums of parish life where no one seems interested are replaced with the high winds of keen interest in lifelong faith formation.

THE CHALLENGE FOR THE PARISH

Now to our point here regarding pastoral planning. The wonderful initial encounter with Christ, the experience of true conversion, sustained in the community, the kind Herb experienced—*that's what we want for every adult in the church.* When that happens, the rest of the pastoral plan falls into place because the signs of that conversion lead to it. The poor are fed. The lonely are visited. The newcomer is welcomed to the faith. The rejected are loved. The widow, the orphan, and the stranger are taken in. The table is set for all. Everyone has the good news preached to them.

But, as the popes and bishops said above, we cannot assume that everyone in the parish has had this initial encounter with Christ. We cannot assume that conversion is going on around us. We cannot assume that merely because they are baptized, the members of the parish are "in Christ" in this way.

And yet, *we do assume this.* Most parishes have no pastoral plan that addresses conversion. And even fewer have a pastoral plan that addresses how to sustain that conversion throughout one's entire lifetime. Without a vision and plan, this key dimension of parish life often gets ignored. But ignoring it is precisely what Bishop Lucker knew would create a lackluster parish. Without a community of people who have met Christ, given their hearts to him, experienced this conversion, and see the signs of it in their lives, how can we expect them to be financially generous, prayerful, motivated to learn, or willing to volunteer?

We turn next to consider a practical planning approach, one that builds on all we've done as a church over these past fifty years, but one which takes it to the next level, the one envisioned by the church for us. In this plan, we will design 1) ways in which parishes can provide opportunities that open the door for the Spirit to touch hearts and lead people to deep communion with God, and 2) ways in which parishes can help people sustain such a profound conversion in their lives. We will also design 3) ways in which to create a more participatory and welcoming Sunday liturgy, 4) ways in which to provide advanced formation and training for catechists and teachers, and 5) ways to support and encourage households of faith in your parish.

PART TWO

THE PLAN
ITSELF

CHAPTER 4

The First Four Dimensions

Word, Worship, Service, Administration

When someone joins a Catholic parish, there are certain features of the parish pastoral plan that can be assumed to be there. These features have been part of parish life since long before Vatican II. In fact, in this regard the council changed very little about parish structure. There are four such features or dimensions to the parish plan.

WORSHIP AND LITURGY

The first is liturgy. Catholic parishes, like most religious groups, have a regular schedule of liturgies. You can assume it. It's part and parcel of being in a Catholic parish that Mass will be available and open to the public. There may also be a schedule of devotions and other opportunities for shared prayer, or even for private prayer, but when you think about what constitutes a Catholic parish, certainly the fact that the Mass is celebrated often is foremost.

Sometimes when you join a church in another Christian denomination, you have to inquire as to whether it's a "high" or "low" congregation. If it's "high" it will most likely have a weekly communion service, but if it's "low" it probably will only offer a communion service occasionally. But when you join a Catholic parish, you never have to ask at all. You know there will be Mass and there will be communion.

Even in parishes where there is no full-time pastor, or in cases where a lay person or religious sister has taken on the role of leading the parish, having Mass is part of how that parish defines itself. Word and communion services are sometimes held in circumstances where no priest is available, but it really is the Mass that still defines the Catholic parish.

Having liturgy is part of every pastoral plan in every Catholic parish in the world. This, then, forms the first dimension of the parish pastoral plan: worship and liturgy. Here's the beginning of our pastoral plan:

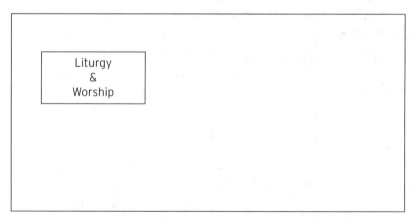

Figure 1: The first dimension of the pastoral plan in today's Catholic parish

Pastoral care

When you join a Catholic parish, you can assume that the pastoral plan will include some level of pastoral care. If you call the parish and ask for someone to bring communion to the sick in the local hospital, or to visit the homebound, or to offer some level of counseling or support in times of need, the parish has a plan to provide that. The Catholic Church celebrates a sacrament in many of these circumstances, the sacrament of anointing.

Some parishes organize this more elaborately than others, with large teams of people trained as "Stephen Ministers" or trained in other methods, to care for people as they age, as they deal with various disabilities, in raising children or providing daycare, and in many other common circumstances of daily life where the support of the parish is needed.

This isn't something optional for parishes. Even if the services that the parish provides are minimal or disorganized, if you are dying and you call for a priest, one will almost always appear.

This is a second aspect of the pastoral plan which is part of every Catholic parish in the world. It's built into our sacramental nature to provide pastoral care. Here, then, is how our pastoral plan is now developing. We have two distinct, yet connected, areas of ministry:

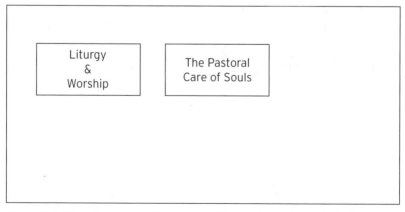

Figure 2: Adding the second dimension of the pastoral plan in today's Catholic parish

BUILDINGS, MONEY, AND ADMINISTRATION

It's also part of the pastoral plan in Catholic parishes to own facilities. It would be a rare Catholic parish indeed that did not own land, at least a church building, a parking lot, and often a school, rectory, social hall, or other parish facilities. And of course, having buildings means needing money. So when you join a Catholic parish, you can pretty much count on the fact that you will receive offertory envelopes with which to make financial contributions. The offertory envelope is part and parcel of parish membership. In many places, it's how we count our people. To be counted as a household within the parish, you have to have envelopes.

Part of the pastoral plan is to administer the money well and carefully, and the universal church governs how this is done in book five of the Code of Canon Law. The parish pastoral council is not, in fact, obligatory. But having a parish finance council *is* required under church law. The pastor really has no choice. He is not free to spend parish money any old way he likes.

And one aspect of managing the funds of the parish well is the care of the poor, the needs of the homeless, the distribution of funds according to the message of the Gospel regarding the Reign of God. It's part and parcel of the pastoral plan of the church that money will be used to further the mission of the Gospel, not enrich anyone personally.

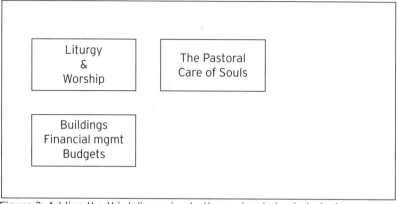

Figure 3: Adding the third dimension to the pastoral plan in today's Catholic parish

EDUCATION, SACRAMENTS, FORMATION

When you join a Catholic parish, you also don't need to inquire whether or not this parish offers catechesis for children. It's part and parcel of parish life that there will be some level of catechetical instruction or formation. Every parish has religious education and someone to coordinate that, even if it's a volunteer. The parish will also offer youngsters and their parents some level of help to get ready to receive Eucharist and reconciliation for the first time. The same is true for confirmation. Every parish has a confirmation program. This is a part of the pastoral plan of the church that one can assume will be available.

Likewise, those preparing to baptize a child or marry can assume that some program of preparation will be available at the local parish. It's part and parcel of Catholic life to do this. Every pastoral plan includes it.

In most parishes, there is also a process for people who are not baptized and wish to be, or who are not in full communion with the church and wish to be. In most places, there is a team of people guiding such journeys of faith through the catechumenate or the Rite of Christian Initiation of Adults (RCIA). Sometimes this ministry finds its home in the parish in the arena of liturgy rather than education, but wherever it is found, one can assume that a person asking to join the church will be offered a process of some kind. It's in the pastoral plan of most parishes of the church.

Many parishes also offer Catholic schools for their children, sometimes for children in grades kindergarten through high school, but more often at least kindergarten through sixth or eighth grade. Having a school is not part of every parish's pastoral plan, but having religious education at some level for children is. You can assume it.

And, increasingly, parishes are also offering adults some level of faith formation, either Bible study or information nights or seasonal preparation evenings before Advent and Lent. Many parishes also offer family-based formation opportunities. In any case, you can count on a Catholic parish to do this. It's part of the pastoral plan.

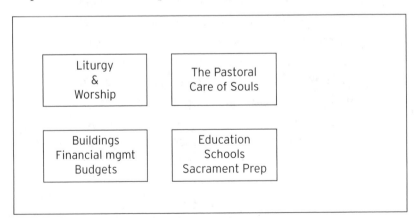

Figure 4: Adding the fourth dimension to the pastoral plan in today's Catholic parish

Most parishes have a pastoral plan that resembles the diagram in Figure 4. Over the years, they have developed a four-fold overarching plan, which include ministries of the word, worship, service, and administration. Their pastoral plan is shaped around these four, and their budget reflects them as well. Most other smaller areas of ministry find their home within one of these four major groups.

Some parishes add other major areas as well, such as hospitality, or daycare, or others. But in general, this is the pastoral plan of most parishes in the modern church. This is, as we said earlier, essentially the same pastoral plan that the church had in the 1950s, on the eve of Vatican II. We Catholics have always provided liturgy and sacraments, education, administration, and pastoral care. Always.

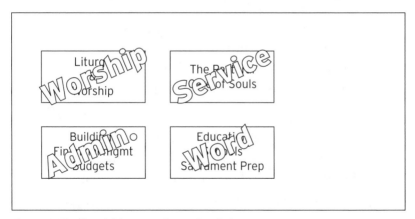

Figure 5: The fourfold areas of a pastoral plan

WHAT'S MISSING IN THIS PICTURE?

What's missing, of course, are those two elements of which we spoke in the last chapter, the ones for which the popes, bishops, and other church leaders have been calling for three or four decades: 1) opportunities for folks to experience conversion to Christ, and 2) a way to sustain that conversion in the life of the community.

It's never quite this black and white, however. There is some conversion being experienced in the current pastoral plan. Certainly in the RCIA, catechumens are being offered chances for faith sharing and other moments which lead them to know Christ. In religious ed programs, faithful catechists and their leaders are providing retreats and other opportunities for conversion. In pastoral care, around the bedside of a dying loved one, the compassion of a parish minister touches hearts and leads them nearer to Christ. Youth ministry has always had retreats and other conversion experiences foremost in their planning.

It's not that the current pastoral plan is failing. Most parishes today *are very good parishes.* But to become a truly great parish, pastoral planning must look beyond the current four-fold structure. Why? Because there is general consensus among the pastoral workers of the church today about the following:

✛ Many people just aren't enthusiastic about their faith.

✛ Many others are just meeting the minimum requirements in order to get a baby baptized or in order to be able to use the church building for a wedding.

✛ Many parents just don't seem to want a role in their own children's faith formation, or don't know how to take such a role.

✛ There seems to be a sort of lukewarm response to the Mass. People don't sing out with full voice. They mutter the responses or don't respond at all.

✛ Mass attendance seems low. In fact, from the peak weekly Mass attendance among U.S. Catholics in 1958 (74%) it is down to just 40% in 2003 (Gallup poll 1939-2003). The church's own polls put that number even lower.

✣ Anecdotal feedback suggests that as many as sixty or seventy percent of parents with a child in religious ed or a Catholic school are not themselves actively taking part in weekly Mass or other activities in parish life.

✣ It's very hard to get enough volunteers sometimes just to meet the needs of the current programs.

✣ Collections should be higher. Catholics are giving at the lowest rate per person of all Christian denominations according to Gallup polling.

✣ Adult members of the parish just don't show up for adult faith formation offerings. They don't seem interested. Even when those offerings are truly excellent and well planned only a small number take part.

✣ There's just no fire in the belly of the parish!

How can we light a fire within the parish? How can a pastoral plan help reinvigorate and reenergize parish life? What must we do to get people excited again? How can our dreams and visions for the parish become reality?

Answers to questions like these are never simple. But there is a powerful and effective way that you can plan for and carry out a method to start down this road. The next three chapters will explore this. The final chapter discusses how to create the team within the parish to succeed at this and become a truly great parish.

Reflection Pause here and talk with other parishioners about the state of life in your parish. How closely does it match what is described above? Make a two-column list. On one side, list all the parish strengths and assets. On the other, list the challenges you face.

CHAPTER 5

The Fifth Dimension

Opportunities for Deeper Communion with God

We know that we simply can't send everyone off to make a Cursillo, like Herb did. There simply aren't enough Cursillo centers, and besides, Cursillo is not for everyone. Some people would simply never attend such a retreat, and others would find it unsuited to them.

But we also know that we can get virtually the same results by hosting a variety of opportunities right at the parish. What kind of opportunities?

✠ Parish-based retreats or other times of encounter with Christ

✠ Times for faith sharing

✠ A method to study the faith that includes more than learning, but also group conversation to help deepen faith

✠ Work for justice, efforts to ease suffering among the poor, or for other social causes, which includes a pause at the end to peer into the experience and see how God's hand was present in it.

Sometimes, such opportunities may be shared among several parishes if the parishes are smaller. What they have in common is that these opportunities can provide people with that very important *initial encounter with Christ* and bring them into deeper communion with God. This doesn't happen overnight. Pastoral planners should launch the process and allow it to take the time it needs to unfold, which will be years, not months. There is no magic process that meets every need, but there are multiple avenues, all leading to our Core Work: which is to help people deepen their communion with Christ and sustain that through the church.

We need to build opportunities for conversion, therefore, into the parish plan, and we should treat them in the budget and parish activity on a par with worship, education, pastoral care, and administration. They should, in a word, become part and parcel of the parish pastoral plan. (This isn't the final dimension we want to add to that plan; there is one more which we will consider next.) But for now, this is how the plan might look:

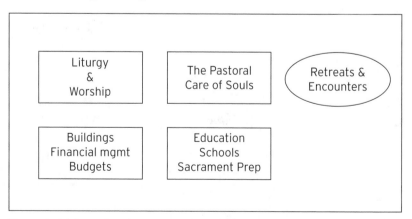

Figure 6: Adding retreats and encounters to the pastoral plan in today's Catholic parish

PARISH-BASED RETREATS

For example, what if your parish offered a parish-based retreat that included the following:

✢ is relatively easy to provide

✢ would cost very little

✢ attracted people to it by its design and content

✢ would be offered for Catholics and their spouses or partners, whether or not both were Catholic

✢ could be offered once a month

✢ was based right at the parish

✢ is held on Thursday and Friday evenings and Saturday morning only until noon

✢ was hosted and offered by a team from your own parish

✢ had as its main goal to help folks deepen their communion with Christ

✢ included the sacrament of reconciliation on Friday evening

✢ and closed with a special retreat Eucharist on Saturday at noon?

Such a retreat exists. It's called "Living Christ!" and it's everything as described just above. All the schedules, to-do check lists, talk outlines, prayer services, handouts, and other aspects of it have been carefully worked out and tested in real parishes and it's currently in use in thousands of parishes around the world, in both English and Spanish. And it's practically free. The publisher of the materials has generously granted permission for you to photocopy all the materials for use within your own parish. To

obtain a copy, simply visit the pastoral planning Web site and download it.

Parishes find that holding one "Living Christ!" retreat per month provides a regular schedule that allows people to plan for it in their busy lives. The regular schedule helps serve people whose life schedules are complex. Many parishes offering this retreat also provide child care or help with in-home babysitting as needed.

Adopting this retreat would provide you with a great tool for many purposes.

To get your copy of the "Living Christ!" retreat, or to connect with other parishes who are already using the "Living Christ!" retreat, visit the pastoral planning Web site at **www. PastoralPlanning. com** and click on "retreats."

✦ It could be a process into which you invite parish leaders, to help insure that their communion with God is as strong as their love for the church.

✦ You could invite couples bringing their child for baptism to first deepen their own engagement with Christ, to have what might be their own initial encounter of faith. Just imagine how this would change infant baptism in your parish!

✦ Couples preparing for marriage could be invited to set aside the time during their period of preparation to share an encounter with Christ as they get ready to make this large commitment together.

✦ Candidates for full communion, especially those whose spouses are active and who may themselves have been semi-active for many years would find such a retreat a valuable way to share the Catholic faith more intensely with their spouse.

✣ This retreat would provide parish youth with energy and excitement about their faith! Many young people have already experienced such encounters and are able to assist the parish in implementing this retreat.

✣ The parish staff could make such a retreat annually with parishioners, sharing the journey of faith and growing as a community. (This would prevent them from becoming the shoemaker's children who go barefoot.)

✣ Liturgical ministers and those doing pastoral care, catechists, Catholic school teachers, youth ministry volunteers, and many others in the parish could use such a retreat to deepen the faith they share with others. What a powerful way to strengthen these ministries!

✣ Perhaps the most important reason for having a parish-based retreat is that it provides "an avenue leading home" for those many people who have been absent from the regular parish activities for a while. Because it begins by tracing each person's journey of faith, includes the sacrament of reconciliation, and ends with Eucharist, it offers a viable way for the ones who feel unwelcome now, or those who are simply absent, to find their way back in peace.

✣ And many others would find this parish-based retreat doable, enjoyable, and powerful.

THE BOTTOM LINE

In order for us to succeed in inviting people into deeper communion with God and an initial moment of conversion to Christ, it is necessary to build opportunities for encounters with Christ *into parish life*. Just as we have those fourfold ministries which we just discussed: worship, education, pastoral care, and administration, we also need an area of ministry that deepens spirituality, which we will call "Retreats and Encounters." If this new program area were added, then someone joining your parish would understand that just as they must 1) learn the schedule of liturgies, 2) the plan for religious education, 3) how to contribute financially, and 4) how to call for pastoral care when needed, they must also now 5) become familiar with opportunities for encountering Christ and plan to take part in them. It becomes part and parcel of parish life.

If opportunities for conversion are not an integral part of parish life, but only a mere add-on, they will be viewed as optional and not as central and essential. And even though conversion does occur within all the other ministries of the parish, it's also true that for most people, conversion results

―――――――――――――∽◯◯◯∼――――――――――――

Our Core Work: Remember, the pathway to being a great parish always keeps you on the same road toward the Core Work of the church: helping people deepen their communion with Christ. This lights a fire in their hearts. Many hearts on fire lead to an active, engaged parish. An active parish has more volunteers, more money, and is more likely to reach out into the community around it to feed the poor and care for the rejected. The more the parish does this, the more people are attracted to it, like to a magnet. They enter, deepen their own communion with Christ, join the others who have done that, become active, reach out, and the circle continues. That's our Core Work. Anything that distracts us from that should be eliminated in our pastoral planning.

―――――――――――――∽◯◯◯∼――――――――――――

from setting aside the time to attend such a retreat and purposefully take this strong step on the journey of faith.

The urgency for such pastoral planning is quite real. Returning to Bishop Ray Lucker for a moment:

> The idea of faith calling us to respond as a whole being has become central in my ministry. The biggest single problem facing the church today is that we have so many people who call themselves Christians but who don't really believe, who haven't in their adult lives made an adult commitment of faith. (Bishop Lucker in 1985)

RETREATS AND ENCOUNTERS

Retreat. The most powerful method for this is the parish-based retreat that we just described above. It's easy to provide, inexpensive, and highly effective.

Other retreats. There are also other excellent parish-based retreats, including Christ Renews His Parish, Koinonia, and offerings from local retreat centers within local dioceses.

Non-retreat Encounters. There will always be a group of folks in your parish for whom making a retreat is just not right. They prefer other, less intense ways of growing in faith. So in the pastoral plan, it is wise to include some other opportunities for encounter with Christ, and one good one is Alpha for Catholics. Others include RENEW, Life in the Spirit Seminars, and others. Gathering adults and young people to pray together, to share Scripture, to share their faith, to share meals, and to grow in the love of Jesus is the key.

Growing Faith Communities. These are a new option for pastoral planning that have emerged in the past three years. *Growing Faith Project* is a resource around which small communities of many kinds can gather to both share faith and learn about the church. It has these features:

For more information about retreats and encounters of various kinds, including the ones mentioned here, visit the pastoral planning Web site at **www. PastoralPlanning. com** and click on "retreats."

✛ It presents the entire *Catechism of the Catholic Church* in plain, understandable English. And it is beautifully laid out with original artwork, in user-friendly booklets, each eight pages in length and each reviewing a specific section of the *Catechism*.

✛ *Y es disponible también en español. Se llama* Creciendo en la Fe.

✛ It's "just the *Catechism*" with no commentary or editorializing, and it has a full Imprimatur.

✛ It has *built-in* faith sharing and shared reflections that provide a powerful avenue for growing in communion with God and the church.

✛ Users form small communities for learning and conversion.

✛ Parishes add this dimension to existing small groups within the parish.

For more on **Growing Faith Project** and how to use it, visit the pastoral planning Web site at **www.PastoralPlanning.com** and click on "Growing Faith."

✛ It is correlated to every children's textbook series in the market.

✛ It is also correlated to the liturgical year, providing a beautiful way to move through the seasons while both 1) growing in one's understanding of the faith and sharing that faith, 2) entering into deeper communion with Christ.

✛ And it is correlated to the new adult catechism now in use in the United States.

✛ It is the perfect learning tool for confirmation candidates, catechumens, candidates for full communion, and others on a journey of faith.

✛ Likewise, part of your pastoral planning will be for a variety of existing groups that already meet within the parish. As you formulate your plan, consult with each of these groups to design a plan with them:

- Parents with children in religious education or the school

- Ministers of various kinds within the parish who wish to grow in their own faith and understanding

- Private use for those who don't want to join a group

- Small Christian communities

- Parish leaders, by adding to existing meetings

- Catechists and teachers

✛ Growing-Faith Communities allow you to do strong pastoral planning in concrete, specific ways, to reach into every corner of parish life with a tool for faith sharing and understanding.

The Question of the Week. In the pastoral planning, you also want to plan for other faith sharing opportunities within the parish. One of these is an ancient practice of the church, used in the catechumenate, called "Breaking Open the Word." In this practice, those preparing for baptism pause after Sunday's Liturgy of the Word and spend time considering the Scripture readings in more depth. They re-proclaim parts of them and then, literally, *break them open,* looking both into the text and into their own lives to find and share the connections. This powerful experience opens the door to the Holy Spirit who moves in their hearts to lead them to deep communion and conversion to Christ.

To find questions for each week of the liturgical year, as well as a simple form to use for helping people use the question in the parish, simply go to **www.PastoralPlanning.com** and click on "Questions." It's all free!

✚ In your pastoral plan, design a method for implanting this ancient practice into the daily and weekly life of everyone in the parish. It will have powerful results, just as it does in the catechumenate itself.

✚ Propose an easy-to-follow "Question of the Week" to help folks break into the texts of Scripture. Such a question could be sent home in a weekly bulletin insert, posted on parish web sites, and used at every gathering and meeting, including education classes, throughout the week.

✚ You must also build into your pastoral plan some method to teach people how to do this. For many Catholics, such faith sharing based on Scripture is new. If possible, the pastor or another member of the parish could model such sharing after the communion rite at Sunday Mass.

✚ Be sure to model brevity. Such faith sharing, when added to existing meetings and events, will surely fail if people believe it is an opportunity to homilize. (There is a strong difference between a homily and faith sharing. The former is about the text. The latter is about the personal faith of the believer.)

✚ A sample faith-sharing guide to use for this purpose can be downloaded from the pastoral planning Web site and is reproducible. There is also a guide there for use in Catholic schools.

More mystagogy. Another powerful way to provide for encounters with Christ and the community is to provide more opportunities in your pastoral plan when folks can simply pause, look back over recent events, and do mystagogy. This could be based on events from people's daily lives or on experiences of liturgy or on other moments in parish life. Here is a method for using mystagogy more widely in parish life:

✚ Learn about it yourself!

  • Mystagogy is a practice that leaders must have embedded in their own hearts and souls.

  • You learn it mainly by doing it with a gifted leader.

  • Find opportunities for this yourself, or host a workshop on it for your parish.

✠ Watch for opportunities to offer it.

• The right moment can't always be planned too far ahead.

• But after certain events or experiences, you can invite the group to pause and step into the process of sharing.

✠ Just ask the questions.

• There are no right answers in mystagogy.

• We are listening to hear how the Spirit has touched the hearts of our community members, so just ask the questions and let the people do the talking.

• Avoid saying too much yourself.

✠ Always end this with a prayer of gratitude.

• When all have spoken and a bit of silence has crept into the process, without fanfare or announcing it beforehand, simply pray aloud about the gratitude which is emerging in everyone's hearts.

• Keep this simple and unencumbered by not homilizing on your part.

✠ Watch people's spirituality grow as a result.

• The more you use mystagogy, the more you will see how it helps folks share in one another's experience, and for many, how it helps them put words on their own experiences.

Working for Justice and Peace, with mystagogy added. In your pastoral planning, design ways for members of the parish to join together to work for justice, either locally or around the world. But be sure to build into such experiences those all-important moments when the group pauses together for the kind of mystagogy we just discussed, to ask the key questions: What happened here, and how was God's hand in this? What touched me personally? Such mystagogy helps consolidate the experience and make explicit the meaning contained within it.

Such work for justice helps Christians experience first-hand the central love Jesus had for the poor. "Whatever you do to the least of these," he taught, "you do to me." Such projects could include:

+ Working among the materially poor

+ Work for peace and the end of war

+ Work for a resolution to the global environmental crisis

+ Help resettle immigrants or refugees

+ Help fight for human rights in every sector of society

CHAPTER 6

The Sixth Dimension

Sustaining the Excitement of Faith

There is another essential aspect to the parish pastoral plan. No one who has a powerful, initial encounter with Christ can long sustain his or her faith without support from the community. Christ is encountered *in community*, not alone. He has chosen to make himself present to us when two or three are gathered, when we join hearts and hands in service together. Because the encounter is a shared experience, the support needed to sustain it must include some shared experiences as well.

For most people, the encounter with Christ is the result of their personal decision to talk about their own lives and the faith dimension of them. It is in *sharing faith* that the heart seems most open to the Spirit. One of the mysteries of our faith is that God has always spoken to us *as a people*. Private revelation is rare. Hence, there is a great need within parish life to have adult Faith Gatherings for support and sustenance.

God is working within us already. The grace of Christ is present. When we become aware of this through prayer, reflection, or insight, sharing it with others *leads us to see it more clearly ourselves.* It's *personal* but not *private.*

Within the parish, designing a pastoral plan that includes opportunities for people to have this initial encounter through the ways we described in the previous chapter is certainly vital (retreats, encounters, mystagogy, working for justice, and so forth). But equally vital is the need to expand the pastoral plan a bit further, to do the hard work of pastoral planning to design ways in which we can support people afterward. This support certainly could come in a variety of ways: phone calls, personal contact, notes, or e-mail. But the most profound way to offer support to people who are growing in their faith is in the form of an *adult Faith Gathering.* By providing a regular and predictable schedule of such gatherings, you create an avenue down which people can travel together in their journey of faith. And just as there is more than one way to offer the encounter with Christ, so there are several ways for folks to gather later for support and follow-up.

We are now completing our pastoral planning picture, and it looks like this:

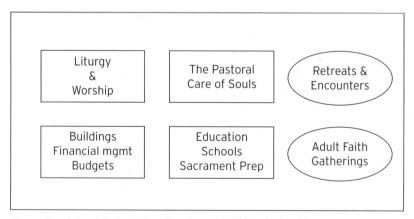

Figure 7: Adding adult Faith Gatherings to the pastoral plan in today's Catholic parish

Recall the old four-square pastoral plan that included those basic areas of word, worship, service, and administration. Figure 7 now adds the two missing elements: 1) retreats and encounters with Christ and 2) adult Faith Gatherings to form and sustain faith. With these added, the original four take on new energy.

There are many excellent resources available today on intergenerational gatherings. See in particular **Generations of Faith** by John Roberto. For more on this, visit the pastoral planning web site at **www. PastoralPlanning. com** and click on "intergenerational."

NOW LET'S ADD A TWIST

Even more powerful, however, than adult Faith Gatherings, may be those that cross lines with the children and youth of the parish. In your pastoral planning, think about holding occasional events that are *intergenerational*. Such events have many advantages because they allow parents and children to share in the same faith experience. And they also allow all those other adults in the parish who have no children of school age to share in them as well.

A SPIRAL SCOPE AND SEQUENCE

Before we go on, there is a very important dimension of pastoral planning that we must turn to here, whether you're planning adult or intergenerational gatherings. As a parish planner, it is worth your time to learn about what is known as a "spiral scope and sequence."

In a spiral scope and sequence, every group in the parish follows the same themes at the same times.

Every textbook series has within it a scope and sequence. The scope is the list of topics and teachings that will be covered for each grade level, and the sequence is the order in which they will be treated. Taken together, they form a curriculum. As you plan for the whole community, including adults, some thought must be given early in the process to what sort of curriculum you will offer adults.

For many years in the church we have almost exclusively offered only children's religious education. The texts we use for this are carefully scrutinized by a committee of bishops, and if they are suitable, they are declared to be "in conformity with the *Catechism of the Catholic Church*." The *Catechism* is the normative source for all Catholic teaching.

But beyond that statement of conformity, there is another dimension to religion texts, one about which the bishops' committee does not render a judgment. And that is the way in which the material is presented and taught. In this regard, each textbook company has its own approach. One approach, the one most effective for our purposes here in pastoral planning, is an approach that permits us to use a single theme across all age levels of the parish. It's called "spiral" because it presents new material each year, based on consistent themes, and the material is presented at an age-appropriate level. Everyone in the parish is thus sharing and learning about the same things at the same time.

In the old linear style of teaching, the students in each grade studied an annual theme that applied only to that particular grade, and they did not return to that theme again over the years of their formation. See Figure 8 for a picture of this. This figure shows the actual themes we have traditionally taught at each grade level. Notice that this plan stops at eighth grade. It's easy to see several problems immediately. First, if only the third grade is studying the church, and each other group in the rest of the parish is off studying its own topic, then it's very difficult to establish parish unity. If the parents study one thing while their children study something else, and a third group is involved in yet another subject, this becomes a very complex pastoral plan to manage well. Plus, no one of these themes really sinks in because there is just too much going on at once.

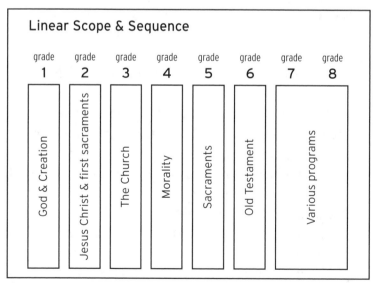

Figure 8: The old silos!

A second problem is also clear. If you only study Christian morality in the fourth grade, and do not return to it each year in an ever more age-appropriate depth (as you would in using a spiral, hence the name), chances are you'll grow up with a fourth-grade understanding of Christian morality.

A third difficulty arises from the fact that this plan addresses mainly the children. Even if there are certain pages to tear out and send home, it's still mainly a children's program. But as we saw earlier in this book, the bishops have asked us to make adult faith formation the central activity of all catechesis, without ever reducing catechesis for children and youth. We can't merely make it an add-on by ripping out a page and sending it home.

But now take a look at Figure 9. Here you see several major improvements. First, all the children still study the same major annual topics, but it's through the lens of the overarching parish-wide theme. In your pastoral planning, this is a beautiful tool. Second, as you can see, this plan is not merely for children. It's for the whole community. So everyone in the parish now has the chance to grow in his or her faith, using the children's program as the springboard. This is very powerful.

And third, because it is spiral, each grade or age level returns to each major topic each year so that a typical learner might have many opportunities at each age of his or her growth to integrate and internalize, for example, an understanding of Jesus Christ. To a first-grade child, this might mean only that "Jesus is our Friend." But by third grade, which is after they have started receiving Eucharist, the child can see a deeper dimension about Christ, asking "what is the Body of Christ?" By sixth grade, the questions are even deeper because in this grade the child is studying the Old Testament and salvation

Spiral Scope and Sequence

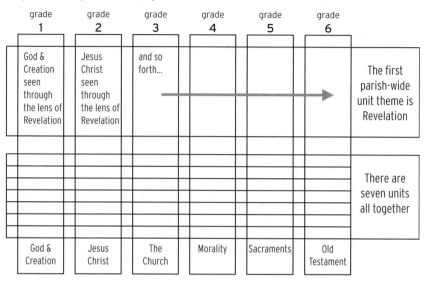

Figure 9: The spiral scope and sequence

history. So now the inquiry into who is Christ centers on him as the fulfillment of the promise to Abraham. In young adulthood, Christ becomes a teacher, guiding choices in life. As a household adds youngsters, the learner is asking how to share about Christ with others, especially one's own children. And in one's maturing years, the questions change again as we grow in Christ and we are now asking about eternal life with Christ, about forgiveness of one's enemies, and the turning of the heart to matters that are important to people in these years of life.

So in a spiral plan, everything is taught just as in the old linear plan, but it's at ever more age-appropriate levels of understanding. The same is true for every topic: morality, prayer, the Trinity, vocations—all of them! But the real strength of the spiral scope and sequence is in having everyone in the parish return to the same themes every year with a parish-wide process for growing faith. By re-visiting our understanding of who Christ is together annually, for example, we grow throughout life. Faith formation is no longer just for the kids; now it's for everyone. We never stop growing.

THE PASTORAL PLAN

With that understanding now, imagine what would happen in your parish if you offered adult Faith Gatherings based on the spiral scope and sequence we have just discussed. Here's how a pastoral plan might unfold:

You could plan to organize such gatherings at the *beginning* of each unit of the children's text. For ease in pastoral planning, let their text be the springboard and roadmap for your plan.

Therefore, one of the primary parish groups for whom you would plan (others will be added later in the pastoral plan!) is the parents and guardians of the children and youth. Asking them to attend one adult gathering per unit is reasonable and results in about seven such gatherings per year. You could also plan an eighth gathering as a closing event scheduled near Pentecost.

And the second parish group you would plan for is those in the parish who have had some form of initial encounter with Christ: a retreat or other encounter experience, those baptized at Easter, or anyone who's had a profound faith experience. These folks bring excellent energy to such Faith Gatherings!

A third group to invite might include the youth of the parish, for whom such encounters are often quite common.

And of course, as soon as possible, begin inviting other parish groups, remembering that the idea is to build this slowly over the next few years. If you want to sustain your growth, it must be built on the solid ground of trial, error, and corrections. This takes time and patience on your part.

What you need

✛ A large room with round tables

✛ Good electronics—a microphone and an LCD projector for PowerPoint

✛ Lights turned down a bit lower than most parish halls

✛ Good music and a way to provide it—live liturgical music is best

✛ Food—the magic key to success

The beauty of the spiral curriculum

Because you're working now on one theme for the whole parish, each Faith Gathering can include everyone, no matter the ages of various children within any one family.

If you gather only adults, the kids could be in their regular classroom settings. But if you gather on an intergenerational basis, all ages and all stages of faith development can share one experience.

These gatherings should "feel"

✠ More like liturgy than school—more like Mass than class.

✠ Full of good, strong energy—a lot of fun, loose, and engaging.

✠ Fun and comfortable. Choose a lead catechist with a sense of humor and good speaking skills. This person can make or break your success at these gatherings. Look for the gift of teaching and the ability to communicate delicate matters with grace and ease.

✠ Interesting and informative, so use media well!

There should be good food, good hospitality, and interaction, almost like a pot-luck supper. Each table should have a designated table leader. These folks do not need a lot of training, but a one-page direction sheet for each gathering or a fifteen-minute rehearsal before getting started is enough. This table leader is key to the comfort of the participants. And remember, many of these parents do not attend Mass on Sundays. They're virtual strangers to us! So the table leader takes on the vital role of being their "first contact." If they like the experience of the Faith Gathering, they may take the first steps to more active participation. But if they're embarrassed or made to feel uncomfortable, if we ask too much from them too quickly, then they will continue to edge away from us. The table leader is the key.

Here are three quick principles to follow when planning for Faith Gatherings of this sort:

✢ They should be on *a regular and predictable schedule* so that people can plan accordingly and make them a priority.

✢ They should really *be fun to be part of.* You can't overdo the fun factor. And by fun I don't mean "playing games," but rather being in a setting where your heart is joyful because of what's happening.

✢ They should *be substantive in terms of content.* Don't offer people fluff. You'll get them once, but they'll never come back. (This is why *Growing Faith* is such a strong resource for these gatherings: it is the full teaching of the church.)

About that food

✢ It's such a key part of all this, don't skip it.

✢ Invite your parish funeral ministers to help, and maybe invite the ushers to serve. They bring the food and stay for the evening.

✢ Or make this into a pot-luck meal if that works in your parish.

✢ But it must be more than a bag of store-bought cookies and a bottle of juice.

A possible schedule for the gathering

7:00   *Gather* with name tags and welcomes all around— remember that many of those attending may not

regularly attend Mass on Sundays, so make them feel
that the church loves them!

+ Have music playing as people arrive.

+ Make sure your welcoming committee finds a spot
for everyone at the table.

7:05 *The Question of the Week*—for six minutes at the
tables. After the sharing is finished, you might invite
two or three to share with the large group. This helps
finish the process and pull it all together.

7:15 *Content Segment.* Each gathering is planned with
the theme in mind, by the lead catechist, parish staff,
or others. The aim here is to help everyone 1) to be
more articulate in their faith on this subject and 2)
to share that faith, opening the door to the Spirit to
touch hearts. Use PowerPoint, film clips, short bits of
live music (such as last Sunday's responsorial psalm),
table projects, large group reporting, or other tools.
But do not lecture people for forty-five minutes or
you'll kill this process. (Remember, you don't have to
invent these gatherings. See the resources segment at
www.PastoralPlanning.com for complete plans.)

8:00 *Break for Food.* You'll need at least fifteen minutes
for this break, maybe longer. The socializing is part
of the process. Play music in the background during
this time to keep the momentum and spirit alive.

8:20 *Sending it Home.* Re-gather the group and focus now
on how people live out what they have just learned
in the content segment.

+ Prepare to send home with everyone a "take home
kit" which has in it items a household needs to live
its faith well and fully. It's not enough to simply

distribute such a kit. You will have to take the time to walk through it and help them see how to use it.

✛ Also send home an invitation to next Sunday's liturgy. Let people know that no matter what they are welcome there.

8:45 *Winding Down.* Before quitting, pause to ask each table to have one more faith-sharing moment in response to this question: "What did you hear or see tonight that you wish to take away with you? What touched you?" After the small group sharing, invite sharing in the large group as well, as much as you have time for.

✛ End with a simple blessing and a "kiss of peace."

✛ Send folks on their way, but don't hurry them out the door. Let them linger if they wish.

✛ Have music playing as people are leaving.

Who attends such gatherings?

✛ As we said, the parents with kids in the religious ed program or parish school.

✛ The newly baptized, newly received into the church, and new members of the parish. What a great way to meet other parishioners! Many times the newly baptized, after a heady and powerful lenten experience culminating in the Easter Vigil, have a hard time finding a community in the parish to sustain their faith. This is it!

✛ All parish leaders. You may need to combine parish business meetings into one night of the month, a single "meeting night," to prevent having too many activities for your leaders. Amazingly, the church will go on even if we have fewer meetings!

For more on resources, either pre-published or designed by you, visit the pastoral planning Web site at **www.PastoralPlanning.com** and click on "resources."

✤ Volunteer ministers—liturgical, catechetical, school, youth, pastoral care, justice, and peace.

✤ Folks who have just made a retreat or other encounter experience.

✤ The parish staff, including the pastor, who takes his place at one of the tables along with everyone else. Do not allow your staff to simply float along the edges of the room. They should be the first to model that we all need deeper communion with Christ and the church.

✤ Invite the morning Mass crowd, the money-counters, and others in the parish who might not have children or be otherwise connected.

✤ Youth and young adults of all ages and stages.

Materials and handouts

There are many resources and materials available now for such gatherings, which are very well done and widely used. See the pastoral planning Web site.

Another option is to create your own, using web based services to design and print precisely what you need.

Languages

These Faith Gatherings can be held in bilingual fashion, but it's really difficult to have more than two languages. If you have a large enough community of folks for each language group, take that route. But it's always best to keep the parish together and mainstream everyone, being sensitive to language needs.

The schedule and curriculum

If you hold one of these Faith Gatherings at the beginning of each unit of the children's book, your curriculum is already done for you! How easy!

✛ *Growing Faith Project* is correlated to whatever textbook you're using. See the Web site for more on that.

✛ Figure 10 shows a possible annual calendar you can follow in order to schedule these gatherings.

✛ Having them occur on a regular basis will help insure success. You can steer into them:

- Couples preparing for matrimony
- Couples preparing for the baptism of their child
- Folks asking for full communion

The Annual Calendar for Faith Gatherings
in a typical parish

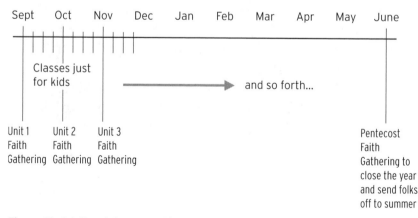

Figure 10: Adult or intergenerational Faith Gatherings

- People who are just starting to make their way back to fuller participation in parish life, but who aren't quite ready for a retreat
- And all the people listed above.

Having such Faith Gatherings, whether for adults alone, or on an intergenerational basis, provides people a place to assemble to sustain their faith and keep it strong, but also to grow in their faith and expand their horizons. For us Catholics right now, this is very important. Many Catholics are involved in Bible study or other courses in neighboring evangelical churches. By providing such Faith Gatherings ourselves, we will meet those needs and at the same time help develop a truly, deeply Catholic spirituality. We will build stronger parish communities by engaging our people more fully, which produces more volunteer ministers, more income in the collections, more people representing our beliefs in the market place and society, and more of the poor being cared for by us.

As you write your pastoral plan for this, design it to make it as easy as possible for people to take part. Knowing your geography and make-up as a parish, set the times and locations to make the gatherings convenient. As pastoral planners, part of your job is to be a resource for the church, which doesn't live at the parish campus. The church lives in the apartments, condos, homes, double-wides, farms, and nursing homes in the neighborhood. Your pastoral task is to serve the church there.

CHAPTER 7

Three Essentials in Lifelong Faith Formation

1. PARTICIPATORY AND WELCOMING LITURGY

If you have not recently re-read the *Constitution on the Sacred Liturgy* from the Second Vatican Council, I strongly suggest that you begin your pastoral planning in this area by doing so.

I say this because Vatican II set down certain principles, ideals, and practical norms, which the bishops and popes of the council want us to embrace (article 4). Two of these are paramount for pastoral planners, so let me cite them here, just to refresh all of our memories.

First, in article 11, and this is repeated throughout the document, the fathers of the council say this:

> But in order that the liturgy may be able to produce its full effects it is necessary that the faithful come to it with proper dispositions....Pastors of souls must, therefore, realize that, when the liturgy is celebrated, their obligation goes further than simply ensuring that the laws governing valid and lawful celebration are observed.

⎯⎯⎯ ⤳⟋⟍⤶ ⎯⎯⎯

If you don't have time to read the **Constitution on the Sacred Liturgy** right now, many of the most salient points it makes can be found on the pastoral planning Web site which is at **www.PastoralPlanning.com.** Click on "Vatican II."

⎯⎯⎯ ⤳⟋⟍⤶ ⎯⎯⎯

They must also ensure that the faithful take part fully, aware of what they are doing, actively engaged in the rite, and enriched by it. (Dublin: Dominican Publications. *Vatican Council II.* Austin Flannery OP, ed. p. 123)

Second, as though to make perfectly clear their goals and intentions, the council fathers went a bit further in article 14, where they wrote:

Therefore, we the participants in this Second Vatican Council, propose one guiding principle before all others as we approach the question on restoring and reforming the sacred liturgy. The principle is this: In the restoration and promotion of the sacred liturgy, the full and active participation by all the people is the aim to be considered before all else. (Notre Dame: Ave Maria Press. *Vatican II in Plain English: the Constitutions.* B. Huebsch, 1997, p. 102)

What does this mean for pastoral planning?

In general, those charged with pastoral planning tend to avoid planning in areas liturgical. Feeling perhaps that liturgy is a legal minefield which should not be trod by amateurs, parish planners typically do not address the guiding principle the council set forth, which is how to plan for fuller and more active participation by the faithful, which is, according to the council itself, more important than merely following the rubrics.

But, what if pastoral planners focused on:

For more on how to welcome folks generously, visit the pastoral planning Web site at **www. PastoralPlanning. com** and click on "welcome."

✛ Making sure that people feel as welcome as possible at the Sunday liturgies. Many people today do not feel welcome. They may not have "darkened our doors" in quite some time. Or they may be "living in sin" in the eyes of the church and feel unworthy or unwelcome. Or they may have made certain moral or personal choices that are out of step with the church and they cannot feel reconciled. And yet, they hunger to come home. How can pastoral planners welcome them wholeheartedly? How can your parish help them see that the church loves them, that they belong to us *because they belong to Christ*—no matter what?

✛ Establishing a way for the community to pray publicly for the matters that are most on the minds of parishioners. Whether at the prayer of the faithful, or at other points in public prayer, even outside of Mass, this would be a way for more active participation.

✛ Planning ways in which the parish can together experience mystagogy each week. Every single week, various pastoral workers, whether paid or volunteer, already visit the sick, counsel the dying, bring joy to the homebound, prisoners, or the grieving, or engage in a variety of other ministries. How can their stories be shared and told in public? How can the messages from those who are absent for these or other reasons become part of the whole community story? This is a powerful way to engage the parish!

✛ Planning ways in which the whole community, assembled on Sunday for Mass, can pray the Eucharistic prayer with the priest. Without causing confusion or breaking any rules, how can this high moment of the parish week become more powerful for everyone?

✛ Making the offertory procession a "real" procession. Does it represent the gifts of the people sitting in those pews each week? How can you do pastoral planning to help this important moment take on new meaning? If the financial gifts being given at this point in the Mass are to be meaningful at all, their presentation must involve everyone. What if each person brought his or her own gift forward, for example, in a sort of messy, semi-spontaneous procession of givers?

✛ Helping everyone who attends this liturgy feel they are welcome to come forward in the communion procession, even if they are not able or choose not to receive communion with us. Pastoral planners can work with liturgists to make this key moment in the week more welcoming and more a real celebration of the presence of Christ.

✛ At the end of Mass, helping people really feel sent. I mean, SENT! out to the world, to love and serve. Is this dismissal a lost moment, or is there a way that in pastoral planning, people could be sent to their schools, jobs, homes, or other daily places with a real mission?

✛ And as people leave, encouraging them to take with them the Scripture readings. Pastoral planners can design ways to effectively send home the Word each week, to help folks break it open and make it part of their own lives, as we discussed above.

Meeting the goals of Vatican II for full, active participation is one of the most important goals for parish pastoral planners. It's a key, essential element of whole community catechesis.

2. FORMATION FOR CATECHISTS AND TEACHERS

It goes without saying that the heart and soul of a successful parish plan for whole community catechesis is based on having spiritually deep, knowledgeable, and capable teachers and catechists. Therefore, having a process through which to form them should be part of the pastoral plan in every parish and school.

There's a "hole" in my parish

In the old days, we had the sisters and brothers in our schools. When we built our Catholic schools, the atmosphere and spirit of those schools was largely established by the presence of religious communities. They prayed together daily and they lived the vowed life. And the spirit of their communities spread into their daily work as teachers. The formation the sisters and brothers received was thus transferred into the classrooms.

What made our schools so "Catholic" in nature was not their names (St. Mark's or St. Anne's) or even their presence within the parish, but the strong lived faith of the faculty and staff.

But today the situation has changed. Our schools are staffed mainly by lay persons, who come and go from daily life very differently than the sisters and brothers did. They are not in formation, and they aren't bringing the charism and spirit of a religious congregation into the hallways and classrooms of our schools. It isn't that our lay staff is unfaithful or of poor heart, or even that they aren't capable. But without the ongoing formation provided by religious life, it's very hard for our schools to maintain that deep, profound, Catholic character and atmosphere. So today there's a sort of "hole" in our parish or in our school. Something's missing. And what's missing is that community spirit with which our parishes and schools were filled.

With this challenge in mind, we must do the pastoral planning needed to replace that missing spirit, to fill in the "hole." The elements to such a plan will include:

✚ *Creating community.* The process of creating community within a faculty or in a group of parish volunteers is very similar to all that we've been talking about in this book. A sense of community emerges as people share their faith. So our pastoral plan should include elements of faith sharing, prayer, and other steps that help create a sense of community.

✚ *Developing a deep spirituality.* As we form catechists and teachers in spirituality, we must take care to help them develop deep and personal communion with God. How can a teacher transfer his or her own faith to the classroom if that faith is not founded on personal conversion?

✚ *Being knowledgeable about the faith.* Here again, just as we prepare a pastoral plan to assist others in the parish to be articulate in the teachings of the church and the Scriptures, so we must offer catechists and teachers no less.

✣ *Having the skills to teach.* The abilities needed for an effective classroom experience in faith formation include things such as how to lead faith sharing, how to teach specific Catholic topics, and how to mentor others in prayer. This isn't the same skill set needed to teach reading or math. The method of teaching should be the one recommended in the *General Directory for Catechesis*, namely that the teachers and catechists learn with the very method with which they will also teach. In other words, they learn how to transfer to the classroom or teaching situation the very substance of their own formation, just as the sisters and brothers did.

A new resource

As we've seen above, having the right resource can mean success or failure in pastoral planning. All the good planning and intention in the world (or in heaven!) won't help if you don't have the resources to support it. Rare is the parish with a staff person capable of writing, designing, and printing every resource the parish needs. And, even if the parish did have such a person, it would quickly become a full-time job.

But what if you were able to find the resource that delivered precisely what you needed for the purpose of teacher and catechist formation? You would be able to form a core community of ministers in your parish, undertaking this four-part formation: community, spirituality, knowledge of the faith, and skills to deliver it. And what if this resource:

✣ Met or exceeded all standards for catechist and teacher formation established by church leaders?

✣ Had a full Imprimatur?

✛ Was designed as a parish or school-based process, yet users could earn university continuing education units by completing it?

✛ Was based on the *General Directory for Catechesis*, the *National Directory for Catechesis*, the *Catechism of the Catholic Church*, and the pedagogy of Christ himself?

✛ Allowed users to experience powerful spiritual exercises, based on the Ignatian Exercises with musical selections to help deepen communion with God?

✛ Helped users learn skills that work in real classrooms? These skills are the very ones needed for effective classroom results, and they are taught with the very method that teachers or catechists will use themselves. They literally "learn by doing."

✛ Helped users could experience a complete review of the content of the Catholic faith, using materials in plain English that will help them transfer this knowledge back to their own learners?

Wouldn't pastoral planning with such a resource be much easier? Well such a process does exist. It's called *Into the Fields. Catechist and Teacher Formation for the Whole Community*. Users form community, share the spiritual exercises, study their faith, and learn the skills needed to pass that faith on—all in the very parish or school where they serve!

There are also other methods and resources for catechist formation, including, of course, *Echoes of Faith* (published jointly by RCL and NCCL). *Echoes* is a well-tested and reliable resource which can easily be used in the context we are describing here. In pastoral planning, the key is to choose the resource which helps you achieve the outcomes you most want, making sure you provide the four-fold process outlined above: community, spirituality, content, and skills.

Who should take part in catechist formation?

✚ Parish catechists who are new to the ministry

✚ Parish catechists who have experience but want or need an update

✚ Members of the catechumenate team

✚ Youth ministers and their volunteer core group

✚ Those who are working in adult catechesis

✚ Those working in sacrament preparation: baptism, marriage, healing, reconciliation, or Eucharist

✚ Others in the parish who are interested

> For more on **Into the Fields** or **Echoes of Faith**, visit the pastoral planning Web site at **www.PastoralPlanning.com** and click on "Catechist."

Getting started with parish catechist formation

When you do your pastoral planning for this area of formation, you'll find that much of the work for organizing catechist formation falls to the parish religious education director along with the pastor. If you plan to provide in-depth formation, it may seem at first as though more work will be on the desk of your parish DRE. In the end, however, with better prepared catechists, the work will be reduced significantly because catechists will:

✚ feel more confident

✚ continue to teach year after year

✣ become a key part of the parish formation team

✣ encourage others to obtain more formation

A key part of pastoral planning for volunteers who are working in a variety of catechetical ministries within the parish is *scheduling*. Design the meeting schedule that works best in your parish. Most parish leaders will invite catechists to one three-hour meeting per month, ten months of the year (skipping July and August). At first, of course, some volunteers will feel that this is asking too much. But as pastoral planners, you must fit this area of formation into the overall new emphasis within the parish of adult formation. We want *every adult* to be growing in his or her faith, including especially those entrusted with teaching. In fact, as pastoral planners, you may have to confront the reality that as parish leaders:

✣ We usually tend to ask for too little in terms of formation.

✣ Many catechists dearly want training. They often, in fact, feel under-qualified for what we're asking them to do.

✣ Not everyone will sign up for this formation, but if you wait until everyone is ready, you'll never accomplish it. So start with "the willing" and take it from there.

✣ Invite youth ministers, catechumenate team members, marriage prep folks, baptism preparation volunteers, and others working in catechetical ministries to take part, too. Forming community needn't be limited to one or another area of ministry.

✣ Work closely with the school in your parish if you have one. Why not include all the teachers and catechists in one formation process? It brings unity to the whole parish and, in the end, we want all school and parish parents to be in our adult or intergenerational Faith Gatherings.

Who should take part in Catholic School Formation?

✛ Every teacher who is responsible for helping to pass on the Catholic faith to the students, including coaches and others who often have the greatest impact on children

✛ Every aide who assists those teachers, especially if they work in any class where religion is taught or where Christian formation is underway

✛ Volunteer parents who assist in the religion program

✛ School staff who have not recently had any Catholic updating or formation

✛ Include all non-Catholic staff members in this process. You'll find that it's very ecumenically friendly.

✛ Work closely with the parish director of religious education and the pastor to avoid duplication and to coordinate more fully.

Getting started with teacher formation

Once again, in the school as in the parish, as you do the pastoral planning, you'll find that much of the work for organizing teacher formation falls to the school principal, religion department head if you have one, and the pastor. And, as in the parish, at first it seems as though more work will be on the desks of your key leaders. In the end, however, with better prepared teachers the work will be reduced significantly.

✛ They will feel more confident teaching religion in the classroom.

✛ More teachers will want to keep teaching from year to year.

✛ You can count on trained teachers for more help in your school.

✛ They become a key part of your team.

✛ They encourage others to obtain more formation.

✛ The overall quality of your program rises and you become a more truly "Catholic" school!

Just as on the parish side, scheduling time for teacher formation in your school calendar is a real challenge. Here are some excellent planning tips:

✛ Choose the meeting schedule that works best in your school. Most principals will invite teachers to one three-hour meeting per month, ten months in the year (skipping July and August), or to five in-service days per year, each day with two *Into the Fields* sessions.

✛ As pastoral planners, you will have to help the principal make it clear that we must ask for more formation from our faculty. We are a Catholic school after all. And to fill in that "hole" left by the absence of a religious community of women or men, the formation of the faculty becomes very important.

✛ Many teachers dearly want training. Like parish catechists, that third grade teacher, for example, may have attended a Catholic college (or maybe not) but had only two courses in religion, both required. One may have been "Yoga for Christians" and the other, "World Religions." So now here he or she is, trying to serve as teacher and catechist for the third grade in your school, but knowing that he or she needs more help.

✛ Just as we said above about the parish, you will never sign up every staff person in your school for this, but if you wait until everyone is ready, you'll never get started. And then, how sad for the school community and its future!

✝ Work closely with the catechetical program in your parish. Why not include all the teachers and catechists in one formation process?

3. DEVELOPING HOUSEHOLDS OF FAITH

Parish pastoral planning doesn't stop at the church door. The goal of the church is actually *not* merely to develop splendid, effective parishes. The goal is to animate the world with the Spirit of Christ. And the church does that mainly by helping grow and develop households of faith.

No matter how well we do at teaching elementary age children about their faith, if they go home to a household where the faith is not shared or cherished or even believed, who is the real teacher in the end? The parish can plant a seed, yes, but active adult Catholics today nearly all came from homes where the faith was important. So reaching those households isn't optional. It's mandatory in our pastoral plan if the parish is to succeed.

This requires on the part of the parish staff and the pastoral planners a certain change in thinking. On the part of the parish staff, they must begin to see themselves not as the ones who *do* ministry, but as the ones who facilitate it. Furthermore, parish facilities are not the only place where members of the parish meet—the main place they meet is within their homes. So the task of the parish is to provide households with the resources they need to make those household meetings (more) holy and (more) intentional.

And on the part of pastoral planners, the people of the church must be trusted to explore and live their faith as they see fit. How they live may not fit precisely into what the leaders of the church or parish think is best. It isn't so much that parishioners live in the world and "go to church," but that they *are* the church and take it out to the world.

So for planners, this will mean a change in how we operate as a parish. You should indeed raise expectations for the household, but at the same time, you should not expect them to do it all "your" way. You must allow flexibility, diversity, and various levels of commitment. Not everyone will be fully committed from the start, or even down the line. And you must begin to affirm everyday life—the Spirit is working there most of all! This means you should develop programs that affirm and assist the household. For example:

✛ Why not teach Christian homemaking?

✛ Why don't you include stories from everyday, household life in Sunday homilies?

✛ Why don't you cater to household life whenever possible in terms of scheduling and planning? At the moment, we tend to pull people out of their homes for parish meetings just at those times of day most conducive to deeper family life, such as suppertime.

✛ Why don't you work on an intergenerational basis whenever possible? After all, households and the Sunday liturgy are themselves naturally intergenerational.

The members of the church don't live at the parish, as we said earlier. They live at home. This is where daily prayer, a love for the poor, and the willingness to forgive each other is needed. If all prayer is planned for the parish campus, how will households ever learn to pray? If giving to the poor is done for them through the parish budget, how will households ever learn to do it? If forgiveness, generosity, hospitality, or communion with God aren't sent home, how will people live it in their everyday lives? For pastoral planners, this is the real challenge.

Indeed, the household is *the* place where Christian formation must occur. All our church documents for fifty years have pushed us in this direction. It's time now for pastoral planning to do the hard work of making this a reality.

Here's what the *Declaration on Christian Education* from Vatican II had to say about this:

> Parents are, in fact, the first and foremost educators of their children within a family atmosphere animated with love, providing a well-rounded formation. The family can be called the first school of those social virtues which every society needs. The Christian family is enriched by the grace of the sacrament of matrimony and is the place where children are first taught to know and love God and to know and love their neighbor. Here they come to understand human companionship, here they're introduced into civic life, and here initiated into the parish community. (Notre Dame: Ave Maria Press. *Vatican II in Plain English: the Decrees and Declarations.* Bill Huebsch, 1997, p. 198)

And here's what the *Catechism of the Catholic Church* says about this:

> Parents have the first responsibility for the education of their children. They bear witness to this responsibility first by *creating a home* where tenderness, forgiveness, respect, fidelity, and disinterested service are the rule. (Washington, DC: USCC, Inc. *Catechism of the Catholic Church.* 1994 from article 2223, italics theirs)

And, of course, the *General Directory for Catechesis* agrees. Here's what it has to say:

> The family is defined by Vatican II as a *domestic church....* The family passes on human values in the Christian tradition, and it awakens a sense of God in its youngest members. It teaches the first tentative steps of prayer, it forms the moral conscience, and it teaches human love as a reflection of divine love. Indeed, the catechetics of the home are more witness than teaching, more occasional than systematic, and more daily than structured into periods. (Mystic, CT: *The GDC in Plain English.* Bill Huebsch, 2001, p. 99)

There are some well-established strategies for this, such as sending home prayer kits or affirming household life. But here are three powerful strategies for pastoral planners who are concerned about household life:

✛ First, encourage adult household members to be engaged in the "retreats and encounters" part of the parish pastoral plan. Help them deepen their own communion with God. Without an initial encounter with Christ, it is nearly impossible for them to sustain faith at home. How can you do this? It will happen mainly person-by-person as those who have made retreats go to their brother and sister-in-law, for example, and tell them how wonderful it is for them to have experienced the retreat. It cannot really be organized by a committee or by a team of household visitors. This person-by-person approach takes time, many years really, which is why planning to host such retreats and encounters is such a high priority for pastoral planners.

✚ Second, create the expectation that each household with children will become part of the adult or intergenerational Faith Gatherings in the parish. This is a chance to grow in a safe, unthreatening environment, even if they're not yet ready to come to Mass every week. The faith sharing and witness or story telling that goes on in these Faith Gatherings also leads to conversion and deeper engagement. If such gatherings are designed as enjoyable and profound at the same time, people will want to attend regularly.

✚ Third, adopt as a parish the "50-50 Partnership Agreements" now in wide use in the church. For more on this, read on.

Partnership Agreements

As pastoral planners, one of your areas of greatest attention must be to the annual time-and-talent sign-up Sunday drive, along with the stewardship commitment Sunday. This process, of convincing members of the parish to be engaged with parish life, is fraught with difficulties, is a real challenge, but also a solvable problem for pastoral planners.

The chief difficulty is that people do not become engaged without having a fire in their hearts for Christ, lit by that initial encounter which we have been discussing. Without that fire, their engagement is lackluster and temporary at best. Hence the suggestion above to make parish encounters part of your plan for growing households of faith.

And this leads to the challenge. How can we help households come to understand their key role in living the faith on a daily basis? The answer lies in the 50-50 Partnership Agreement process.

Possibly the single most ineffective moment of adult catechesis in the entire church year falls on the Sunday when we do time, talent, and treasure "sign up." The pledge cards we use make it seem to people that the only ministry needs about which the parish is concerned are its own. And this leads members of the parish to believe that signing up for sometimes relatively minor ministry tasks around the parish fulfills their full call to live the Gospel and work for the Reign of God.

But, the opposite is actually true!

When parents and children express their love and affection for one another—with notes, hugs, or other signs of kindness, isn't that a moment of honoring their call to parenting? All that's needed is for these acts to become an explicit part of their Christian life. Add them to the pledge cards!

When family members care for each other when sick, notice when someone is lonely, affirm one another for jobs well done, and pay attention to the poor of the world, isn't this part of our Christian call to serve one another? Let these become teaching moments within the household. Add them to the pledge cards!

When a household cares for the environment and recycles, isn't this part of our call to care for the environment? Use these moments to teach about creation and ecology and the connection between the two. Add them to the pledge cards!

When a household decides together how much to contribute to the parish or to the poor outside of parish financial contributions, or to other causes and purposes that benefit society and the world, isn't that part of their overall call to stewardship of money and resources? Add it to the pledge cards!

When a household sits down to a meal together, pausing to enjoy each other and their food, and paying attention to one another's lives, isn't this *the* single most important activity to bring the household together in love? Add it to the pledge cards!

The 50-50 agreements set the stage for living faith in daily life.

When family members forgive each other freely, when reconciliation is a natural part of household life, isn't this the real outcome of the sacrament itself for which we hope? Add it to the pledge cards!

When the members of a household visit an ailing relative, or take a vacation together, or talk explicitly about their faith, isn't this a chance to view what's happening in the world around them with Christian insight?

And yes, of course, when a household is present together in the Sunday Liturgy, volunteers their time at the parish, writes a check for parish needs, or attends Faith Gatherings, this is also part of their Christian call to community.

These are all ways of living that are already underway in many of the households of every single parish. No one has to organize this. All that is needed is to affirm and support it. But how?

Let's make a deal!

Why not enter into a "50-50 Partnership Agreement" with each household of the parish? In such an agreement, the parish promises to do its part, and the household promises to do its share as well. Much of what the parish will promise in such an agreement is already going on at the parish. Likewise, much of what the household will promise in these agreements is also going on. By lifting both sides up into this partnership agreement, by making it explicit in this way, daily life is blessed and parish life is richer.

This is an effective method for making explicit the shared responsibility between parish and household for passing on the faith. Such partnership agreements make it clear that the job of passing on the faith does not belong solely to either the household or the parish, but to both. The job of feeding the poor belongs neither to the households alone, nor to the parish alone, but to both. The same is true for all aspects of the Christian life.

Faith Gatherings are an excellent moment in which to explain and negotiate such agreements. Simply use the gathering to offer members a little catechesis about what the partnership agreements are, a short menu of choices which allows them to write in other items on their own, and time to do the work. A sample of such an agreement can be found on the pastoral planning web site, and is yours to reproduce if you wish.

In preparing partnership agreements, the parish makes some serious promises: to provide religious education classes, a fine Sunday assembly, and an open door to the households they serve. By making such promises, the 50-50 partnership shapes the parish itself, making it more responsive to what the households of the parish need and want in order to live their faith more fully.

Likewise, the household (no matter how it's comprised) makes some serious promises as well: to see the ordinary events of everyday life as holy, to take part in the parish, to make a fair donation of money and time for parish and other charitable or social needs. Hence, the 50-50 partnership also shapes the households and provides ongoing and deep renewal of heart throughout the parish.

Here's an example of what the parish might promise. Any given parish may promise all these things, or some of them, or others which fit into their culture and parish spirit.

✝ As a parish we promise to offer solid preaching and an opportunity for faith sharing based on the Sunday readings every week.

✝ We promise to offer regular retreats and encounter opportunities, and a monthly Faith Gathering, well planned and well coordinated and at no direct cost to the household.

✝ We promise that those who come from your household to the Faith Gatherings will get good instructions about the fundamentals of the Christian faith; we'll use instructional materials that are approved by the local bishop, and we'll provide lead catechists who are well prepared for their work, and who will truly "echo the faith" of their own lives.

✝ From time to time, we'll offer evening or Saturday programs to assist you as a household in living your faith more openly and explicitly, especially during Advent and Lent.

✝ We promise to help you find ways as a household to serve the poor, the rejected, and the suffering—and to coach you to visit the sick, the imprisoned, the lonely, and refugees.

✝ We further promise to make the Sunday liturgy the single most important focal point of parish life. We'll prepare for it carefully and help you as a household to be well disposed for it, ready to participate, and actively engaged in the rites.

✠ We'll welcome you to our Sunday assembly regardless of your situation in life, whether you're single, widowed, divorced, remarried, in an ecumenical or interfaith marriage, gay or lesbian, or sharing a home without marriage; whether you're an immigrant or a newcomer; whether you're fully abled or handicapped, healthy or sick, old or young; whether you're struggling with your faith or firm in your commitment. We'll maintain an open door and an open heart to you, and we'll offer you a share in the grace of Christ which fills this church.

✠ If you call us for help, we'll do everything possible to provide it. If you call with a question, we'll answer promptly. If you ask for prayer, we'll offer it immediately.

And on the other hand, here's an example of what each household might promise. Again, any given household may choose some or all of these or other things not on this sample list that fit into their household culture or spirit.

✠ We promise to become more intentional "home makers" by paying attention to what happens in our home regarding meals, prayer, and time spent together. We will share faith in our household, following the direction given by the Question of the Week in the parish.

✠ We promise to share love openly (exchange love notes, gifts, and other signs of affection) and to pay attention to one another's daily activities.

✠ We promise to have supper together more often, with the TV off, occasionally adding a bit of elegance to our table (candlelight, wine, and flowers). We'll do this at least twice each week, and always on Sundays, or as often as possible.

✛ If there's a quarrel within our household, we promise to work for reconciliation that is explicit and spoken, using the words, "I am sorry" and "I forgive you."

✛ We promise to become more conscious of those people in our family, neighborhood, parish, or wider society whom we dislike or hate; to forgive them for any harm done to us and to find ways to be more tolerant of people we don't like; to gossip less and affirm more.

✛ We promise to become more explicitly conscious of people who are suffering from war, poverty, exploitation, and rejection; to become more aware of those who are sick, imprisoned, on death row, or refugees. And we promise to send a gift of time, food, or money to help ease the burdens of others.

✛ We further promise to make this contribution each week (or month or year) to our parish $_____. And we also promise to support these social causes and charities, and at this amount.

_____ $_____
_____ $_____
_____ $_____

✛ We promise to do at least something to improve our care of the earth on which we live. This might include recycling, picking up trash, going for a hike, or caring for a garden.

✛ We promise to be present and active in the Sunday assembly each week or as often as possible for us, and after Mass to continue to observe Sunday as a "day off" from regular life, to postpone shopping and work as much as possible and try to do something together as a household to extend the celebration of the Mass into the rest of daily life.

✢ We promise to help each other memorize certain prayers and understand what they mean, and to learn about what it means to follow Christ on his Way.

✢ We will attend one retreat each year, and we will attend the monthly Faith Gatherings offered by the parish.

✢ We promise to encourage each other to pray daily and to maintain items within our household which make that possible, such as prayer books, sacred spaces, occasional quiet times, and signs of our faith, and every night before bed we will offer one another a simple blessing: "Good night. God bless you. I love you."

✢ We commit ourselves to volunteer ministry at the parish in the following areas:

_____ and _____.

Parishes that have adopted this approach find that parishioners have a deeper sense that religious education and formation is *their* responsibility whether they're parents, grandparents, neighbors, or parish staff members. Households are affirmed in living a more explicitly Christian life, and parishes are deepened as adults naturally seek more formation for themselves. It's a practical way to implement a whole community catechesis and help form and shape households of faith.

Here's what one parent recently told me about this:

When my two kids came home from religious ed and told me that everyone had to sign up for this 50-50 deal, I said, "No way. That's what we pay them to do down at the church." Looking back now, I'm not sure where I even got that idea. Obviously I've changed my mind after trying it.

My wife, Molly, and I attended the next Faith Gathering in the parish, and we were asked to agree to a 50-50 partnership, so we did. You know, we wanted our kids to know about the church and all. So they showed us this fancy list of things the parish would do. But then the volunteer turned the page and showed us what we could do. The idea of what 50-50 means started to hit home. We looked over that list together and then I looked up at the volunteer and said, "You mean to tell me that by recycling our trash and teaching our kids about it I'm doing part of my fifty percent?"

"Yep," she said. Suddenly it dawned on me. We were already doing a lot of what we had to; we just weren't connecting it to our faith. So we signed up for five or six things and went home. The next Sunday when we had our first family supper under this partnership, I must say, it felt pretty good. Our family was together and it was Sunday and it sort of felt like, I don't know, like a really good thing for us to be doing. And that night, for the first time ever, I sat with my son and we had the TV off and we talked about what it was like when his grandmother died. He actually had lots of questions. I could see how this fit into his understanding of religion. I felt much closer to him than I had for a long time.

It's funny. We live in the same house but we needed this to bring us together.

In the end, as parish pastoral planners, you will see success in your plan as you see more and more households living their faith. So as planners, it's always necessary to keep the household in view. Never replace that with a view of a splendid parish built at the expense of household life.

Interlude

Summary

So far in this book we have considered:

✚ Who you are as a parishioner: a parish leader, a volunteer minister, the pastor, or a parish staff person. Pastoral planning teams comprise a combination of all four.

✚ What the leaders of the church are asking of us, based on the tremendous activity of renewal in catechesis over the past fifty years. This gives us a good idea where we're headed in our pastoral planning.

✚ A strong understanding of what is involved in growing into deeper communion with God. In particular, we came to understand what the initial encounter with Christ is like for people and how they have it—and how that affects our pastoral plan.

✚ A review of the long-standing four-fold framework for pastoral planning, which has been at play in the church for centuries. The four areas are 1) liturgy and worship, 2) pastoral care, 3) ministries of the Word, including schools and sacrament preparation, and 4) finance, stewardship, and administration.

✛ Then we began to consider the practical work of adding two more dimensions to the pastoral plan. The first new dimension is based on the call of church leaders to provide opportunities for conversion, for deeper communion with Christ. We discussed adding a whole new dimension to parish life, on a par with children's catechesis, liturgy, pastoral care, and finance. We called this new dimension "retreats and encounters."

✛ And we also discussed the need to sustain that conversion experience for adults in the church. Here we discussed the need to plan for powerful adult or intergenerational Faith Gatherings. Again, in pastoral planning we would add these as a new dimension as well, on a par with children's catechesis, liturgy, pastoral care, and finance.

✛ We then turned our attention to certain other essential areas of pastoral planning, including 1) making Sunday Mass the absolute center of all we do by planning for more participatory and welcoming liturgies, 2) planning to provide strong, effective formation for catechists and teachers, and finally, 3) developing households of faith as the ultimate goal of the parish.

✛ Next and last, we will turn our attention to the pastoral planning organization needed to do all this work. Here we will see that much is already happening in most parishes. We will also see that once organized, such a pastoral planning team becomes a strong force in parish life.

PART THREE

GETTING IT DONE

Chapter 8

Writing the Pastoral Plan

Dreams and Visions

Change is not easy for anyone. Once we land upon a way of doing things, even when better ways come along, it can be threatening and difficult to shift our methods and adopt improvements. We sometimes almost prefer to struggle along the known pathway than risk a new road with potential dangers. "'Tis better to suffer the ills that we have," Shakespeare wrote once, "than to fly to those that we know not of."

And yet, God's promise is that all things are *new* in Christ. It is a new heart and new mind that the Spirit gives us. We sometimes come to believe that God is ageless, by which we mean to say that God is infinitely old. But in fact, God is infinitely young! The modernity of God is what leads us to new places and promised lands. Throughout history, God has challenged people to have new hearts and new spirits. The Scriptures call us constantly to undergo *metanoia*, another powerful word derived from the Greek, which means *change*. We are called to be forever new in the Spirit, forever open to changing for the better!

So, as we said in the introduction, to move from being a very good parish to being one that is really *great* requires us to change and adapt. And remember, being a *great* parish will produce unexpected results! The people we touch through our planning will go on from here to establish the Reign of God. They will announce good news to hopeless people. They will work to end injustice, to bring about lasting peace, and to introduce others to the one whose grace is in us all, Jesus Christ.

To begin with, as you gather a team of planners or are part of such a team yourself, keep in mind that we are earthen vessels. It is God's Spirit working through us and within us that drives the process into which we are entering. Prepare to become a channel of grace, to set up opportunities for yourself and others through which the amazing power of God will work.

Remember in pastoral planning that you are not planning something that *other people* will do in the parish. You are planning for yourself as well, whether you're a staff person, the pastor, a key volunteer, or a long-time parish lay leader. This isn't about *them*. It must be about *us*.

BEFORE YOU BEGIN

At a minimum, everyone involved in planning should be familiar with certain specific resources. The first group of resources listed here includes documents from the popes and bishops, from academic leaders, and parish leaders. This background is important because it helps us see *where we're going together*.

The second group listed below includes resources we will use to implement the plan. Your plan will be realistic only if it is designed to actually work. And what will make it work is having effective resources to use. If your plan is written

"in the dark" without reference to such resources, later, when you try to implement it, you'll be frustrated because the plan itself won't match the tools needed to actually build and drive the parish ministry vehicle.

BACKGROUND RESOURCES

At a minimum, you should be familiar with the following documents.

✦ *The Constitution on the Liturgy* from Vatican II, available in plain English

✦ *The Constitution on the Church* from Vatican II, available in plain English

✦ *On Evangelization Today*, from Pope Paul VI, available online

✦ *On Catechesis in our Time*, from Pope John Paul II, available on-line

Over the past ten years, Catholic publishers have been creating and publishing an array of powerful new resources for lifelong faith formation. While it is not possible here to cite all of them, we have tried to list most of them on the pastoral planning Web site. To read these reviews and even see samples of those products, visit **www.PastoralPlanning.com** and click on "resources."

✦ The *Rite of Christian Initiation of Adults*, the document which restored the catechumenate in 1988. There is a group of documents on the catechumenate, but this one is central to them all.

✦ The *General Directory for Catechesis*, available in plain English

For information on how to obtain these resources, visit the pastoral planning Web site at **www. PastoralPlanning. com.** Click on "background" then select the document you wish to find. Many of these can be downloaded in the language of your choice.

✦ *Our Hearts Were Burning Within Us*, the Leader's Guide (in the United States only, but applicable everywhere), available from the United States Catholic Conference publishing office

✦ *Nurturing Adult Faith* (in the United States only, but applicable everywhere)

✦ The *National Directory for Catechesis* (in the United States only, but applicable everywhere), available from the United States Catholic Conference, publishing office

✦ Various excellent study texts. See the Web site for a full list.

Implementation resources

✦ *The Growing Faith Project*—the entire *Catechism of the Catholic Church* in plain English, presented in modular booklets that can be used as short courses, or as a complete course in the faith. From Twenty-Third Publications and Harcourt Religion Publishers.

✦ *Into the Fields: Catechist and Teacher Formation for the Whole Community*—a powerful formation process that creates a strong community at the heart of the parish, designed for all ministers, especially catechists, teachers, youth ministry workers, and catechumenate team members. From Twenty-Third Publications. Accredited through Loyola University New Orleans.

✢ *Echoes of Faith.* This is a video-and-workbook based process providing excellent background and skills formation for catechists. Published jointly by NCCL and RCL.

✢ *United States Catholic Catechism for Adults* from the United States Catholic Conference. A new and flexible way to become familiar with the full range of Catholic teaching. From the United States Catholic Conference of Bishops.

For information on how to find any of these resources, either online or to purchase, visit the pastoral planning Web site at **www. PastoralPlanning. com.** Click on "implementation" then select the document you wish to find.

✢ *People of Faith: Generations Learning Together*—a new resource that contains everything you need to conduct effective intergenerational Faith Gatherings in your parish, including a CD-ROM with reproducible handouts and prayers. From Harcourt Religion Publishers and the Center for Ministry Development.

✢ *Threshold Bible Study*—a powerful resource organized around *lectio divina* which helps users enter into the texts of Scripture from a thematic point of view. Excellent for small group use. From Twenty-Third Publications.

✢ A variety of books by major figures in the field of lifelong catechesis. See the Web site for the full list. From a variety of publishers.

OUR HEARTS WERE BURNING WITHIN US

The U.S. bishops have provided a powerful and effective planning tool, which is of enormous importance to parish pastoral planners, even if you live outside the United States. It is the *Leader's Guide for Our Hearts Were Burning Within Us*. (It's on the list of resources mentioned above.) Reprinted with permission below is the method for planning that the bishops suggest. (The article numbers from the bishops' document have been retained.) Following that is a simple step-by-step plan to follow their suggestions and write the actual pastoral plan for your parish.

> #168 *The implementation* of this pastoral plan [for adult faith formation] can bring about profound transformation and renewal in our nation, our dioceses, and our parishes. But the plan needs to be embraced first by diocesan and parish leaders, embodied in pastoral structures and services, and put into practice by well-prepared ministers. Here are steps to take to begin this process of implementation.

> #169 1) *Study the plan,* pray about it, and discuss it with others. Take time to explore its vision and initiatives. Discover how you can support the plan and how the plan can support you and others in your various ministries. Commit yourself to its implementation.

> #170 2) *Analyze the situation* in which adults actually live in church and society. Carefully research and assess the current state of affairs in adult faith formation and pastoral life in both parish and diocese. Consider how socio-cultural and economic factors, local needs and resources, the formulation of options, and existing priorities influence the implementation of this plan.

#171 3) *Develop action steps* for implementing the plan. As dioceses and parishes determine their prioritized goals, objectives, and strategies for adult faith formation—flowing from the mission of the church and the analysis of the local situation—an effective plan of action will emerge. The implementation of this plan will be characterized by its realism, simplicity, conciseness, and clarity. Such a plan will set a course for action that will generate enthusiasm within the local church.

#172 *The plan will address the needs of the whole community*, for "the true subject of catechesis is the church." It will do this especially by attending to the various relational networks and populations in the parish. Ultimately, it will reach to the heart and mind of the individual adult and his or her need for primary proclamation, basic catechesis, or continuing education in the faith. When individuals and small communities seek out the formation they need—and when parishes have oriented their ministries to provide it—then adult faith formation will be a true priority.

#173 4) *Prepare your leaders.* Identify, invite, train, and support people to serve as lead agents in fulfilling the plan. All who serve in this ministry, whether full-time professionals, active parishioners, or outside speakers and consultants, need adequate formation.

#178 5) *Make a commitment* of financial resources. It is not enough to talk about the need for adult faith formation; actions are also essential. Budgets and personnel decisions will need to be reconsidered in light of this plan. The challenge will be to provide resources to build adult faith without undermining other educational activities already engaged.

The steps for pastoral planning outlined below follow the bishops' suggestions. Let's get started!

THE PLANNING PROCEDURE

In a nutshell, here is the overall procedure:

1. Decide to do this and commit yourself to the vision and process. Then get the right people to help.

2. Identify and name your Lifelong Formation Coordinator.

3. Identify and gather a *Dreams and Visions* Team.

4. Identify and talk with the specific groups you hope to reach within the parish.

5. Begin forming catechists and teachers for the work ahead.

6. Hold a series of meetings as a *Dreams and Visions* Team over about six months.

7. Prepare a short, written Pastoral Plan document—consider it "in process."

8. Invite each affected group to give you feedback.

9. Slowly begin implementing while continuing to hold monthly team meetings to evaluate and adjust the plan.

10. Keep doing this forever.

IN MORE DETAIL

1. Decide to do this and commit yourself to the vision and process. Then get the right people to help.

The commitment of the pastor and senior staff members, and key volunteers to the *Dreams and Visions* planning procedure is essential. Once you as a staff have reviewed the work of the past fifty years in the church, considered the current needs in your parish, and come to believe in the Core Work of *helping people deepen their communion with Christ and sustain that within the church,* then you must make your first decision.

As parish leaders, your own humility and modesty in sharing this decision with others in the parish will be powerful. By being "the deciders" you do not become "the dominators." It is necessary for you to be firm in your resolve and commitment, however. You yourself must passionately desire the outcomes which the planning for this Core Work will produce. You must be ready to work tirelessly behind the scenes, attributing success to your leaders, but accepting failure as your own responsibility. You won't be the one taking credit for dazzling success! You must also be ready to travel beyond what you know to be the comfortable and familiar territory of being a "good" parish.

A key meeting. When you're ready to do so, hold a key meeting with your top personnel, whether paid or volunteer—or both. In this meeting, make the formal decision to go forward. Mark this as your beginning point and anniversary. Later, when we evaluate and measure outcomes, this will be a key date in your planning process.

The key people. This may not be easy or even possible for you to do alone, which is why having the right team is so essential. So the second step, after your own firm commitment to this is made, is to make sure you've got the right people traveling with you. Therefore, before you even begin the planning process, evaluate your team. Parish teams tend to form accidentally. Some members of the team have been there since "three pastors ago." Others have only just arrived. How long they've served matters less than whether they share in the dreams and visions of being a great parish.

Choosing your Lifelong Formation Coordinator, and other parish staff positions. Human resources in the church can be a real minefield. Hiring people and laying people off is not easy work. But it is important for you to fix firmly in your own mind the importance of having the right people in the right places on the staff. This will make the difference between remaining simply a good parish and becoming truly *great*! Even before the planning begins, *who you have working and planning with you* is far more important than *what they are doing.*

Here again, Jim Collins offers brilliant insights into this whole matter, in chapter three of *Good to Great.* You can have the best plan and strategy in the world for your parish, but if you do not have the right people on the bus, as Jim Collins puts it, you'll never get where you're going. We sometimes think we're doing a favor for those "wrong" people who are already on our staff. We think the charitable thing to do is to give them one more chance, or worse, find ways to have someone else do the tasks they are not capable of doing. But in fact, the charitable thing, and the right thing for the parish, is to help them find the true vocation where they can excel, even if it is outside parish ministry.

Echoing Jim Collins, here are two key principles for you to follow in getting the right people on the bus in your parish. First, if you are interviewing someone but you are still in doubt that this is the right person, wait! Don't hire this person! You can't make an almost-right person into your top leader. Keep looking and the right person will come along. Second, when you know in your gut that it's time to change or end the role of a staff member, check first to be sure they're not simply in the wrong role for you. But if you can see that there is no role for them, invite them "off the bus." Follow all rules of fairness and legal requirements, but don't sabotage your plan with the wrong people. As Jim Collins puts it: "The old adage, 'People are your most important asset' is wrong. People are not your most important asset. The *right* people are" (*Good to Great*: New York: HarperCollins, 2001, p 64).

Discernment about the role and vocation to which we are called in the church must include all the things we are discussing here. We may be placing obstacles in front of the Spirit by failing to choose and form the right group of leaders.

Now, of course, in many smaller and clustered parishes, no such staff people exist in the first place, and all of this work is done by volunteers—or not done at all. It's not a question for you of hiring or firing, but of finding willing folks to step forward. And sometimes, you have to ask them to cross parish lines and serve with you in two or three or even four parishes. Check in at www.pastoralplanning.com for more on this.

2. Identify and name your Lifelong Formation Coordinator.

It is now time to name the leader who will be responsible for implementing this plan, and this person will carry the title, Lifelong Formation Coordinator. Note that in some parishes, this same person may also have responsibility for the children's religious education program. But in most cases, this will have to be a separate role simply because the work load would be too much if they were combined.

This coordinator will most likely be on the parish staff or, if not, receive at least some compensation for his or her work. Working with the team, the coordinator operates as a sort of entrepreneur in the parish, helping to lead and invent the new horizons toward which the pastoral plan will stretch. Other characteristics to look for in this person might include:

✛ Understands whole community catechesis and lifelong faith formation and sees the long horizon. These are not new "programs" to adopt but a new way to structure and organize the parish, centered on our Core Work, which once again *is to help people deepen their communion with Christ and to sustain that in the church.* (I keep repeating the Core Work because everything we do must be oriented around that.)

✛ This person has and can share about his or her deep communion with Christ.

✛ He or she can be inventive, without running off alone in his or her own direction.

✛ Works well with others; is modest and humble, yet driven

✛ Has a strong catechumenate background

✛ Is selfless and generous with time and is able to attend *Dreams and Visions* Team meetings and other gatherings, but at the same time is able to live a healthy, balanced life

✛ Is a very gifted teacher and good communicator

✛ Has a sense of humor, including about him or herself

✛ Has a background, if not a degree, in theology

✛ Is deeply rooted in what is authentically Catholic

✛ Can plan with an eye to ecumenical relations

Part of the job description of the Formation will be:

✛ to carry the designs of the Team forward

✛ to help integrate those designs into parish life

✛ to make sure funding is there in the parish budget

✛ to balance new initiatives with other aspects of parish life

His or her job description might also include:

✛ Convene and coordinate the *Dreams and Visions* Team
  • Stay in constant close communication with the pastor and the rest of the pastoral staff. There should be no surprises for the pastor and senior staff.

✛ Coordinate efforts among the various ministries of the parish, including very practical matters such as schedules and limited resources or the use of building space. This person would do the problem-solving needed from time to time, to keep the plan moving forward. He or she would watch for opportunities in the liturgical calendar, the culture, the neighborhood, and the town, and ask the question, "How can we take advantage of this opportunity?"
  • For example, scheduling the Faith Gatherings (one per unit of the children's book) requires the coordination of the director of religious ed, the principal of the school, the liturgy program of the parish, and the overall parish calendar.
  • For example, creating the communication and marketing needed to reach members of the parish with information about retreats, encounters, Growing-Faith communities, or other adult learning opportunities, requires the coordination of many in the parish,

For more information and ideas about "marketing as a parish practice," see the pastoral planning web site at **www.PastoralPlanning.com** and click on "marketing." If you have a successful marketing story, you can also share it there—and please do!

including some new folks such as writers, designers, marketers, web producers, and others.

✛ He or she would also ask the question, "Who isn't being served?"

✛ This person would also assist in creating the annual calendar and making sure there is space and equipment where needed.

• Space and equipment quickly become two of the biggest challenges we face when we expand catechesis beyond children.

• One excellent source of funding to provide for needed equipment might be fraternal groups such as the Knights of Columbus or the Catholic Daughters of America within the parish who have been generously donating equipment to the church.

✛ This coordinator is also the person who can help keep the parish from being too timid. Starting too slowly is like not starting at all. There may be a time when as a parish, you simply decide that this is the direction and now is the time—so let's get started! Having a great coordinator in place makes that possible.

✛ The coordinator serves as the "great communicator" and would be wise to have an assistant to help with this part of the work. Announcing the Good News is, after all, actually a communications matter. The more effective you are at communicating with the wider parish, the stronger your program will be.

3. Identify and gather a Dreams and Visions Team.

1) Once the pastor and senior staff or key volunteers have made their own firm commitment to the *Dreams and Visions* procedures, and 2) once a person has been identified as the coordinator for it all, it's time to call together a *Dreams and Visions* Team. This is the group who will both plan and implement the vision for lifelong faith formation. Who should be on this team?

✙ The pastor and possibly other priests on the staff

✙ Persons responsible for carrying out the plan

✙ Key volunteers, retired members of the staff who still live in the parish, ministry leaders, and others. You're looking for people who are deeply committed to the dreams and visions of the parish, but without their own agenda. Like the other leaders described here, they should be modest, yet driven.

4. Identify and talk with the specific groups you hope to reach within the parish.

The *Dreams and Visions* Team has two major roles. The first major role (we'll discuss the second role a bit later) is to identify and talk with all the various constituencies within the parish, and have in mind all the various needs and wants of these groups. Much of their work will be to address that body of information. Here is a list of such groups in any given parish. Your specific parish may have more or less.

✙ Parents or guardians who have children in religious ed or the school

✠ Catechumens and candidates for full communion

✠ Those returning to the church after being away a while

✠ Parish council members and members of various parish committees

✠ Catechists, school teachers, and their aides

✠ Lectors and liturgical musicians, the choir

✠ Those with special needs and disabilities

✠ High school youth who are not part of any formal program

✠ Confirmation students

✠ Students on campuses within the parish

✠ Young adults—out of high school but not in the military or school

✠ Baptism prep families

✠ Marriage prep couples

✠ Adults who do not have children in catechesis

✠ Small Christian communities and post RENEW groups

✠ Households of Faith

✠ Folks who will join no groups whatsoever

✠ Maturing adults living in assisted care facilities in the parish

The listening process. It's really important for the members of the *Dreams and Visions* Team to actually meet the members of the parish. Knowing *about* people is very different from being familiar with them in person. This is an ongoing process throughout the work of the years ahead, not something that can be initiated and completed in a month or two. Members of the team make it a point to seek out and talk with the members of the parish as often as possible.

5. *Begin forming catechists and teachers for the work ahead.*

Early in this process, launch a core group of people using *Into the Fields* or *Echoes of Faith* to prepare the catechetical leaders you will need for the new directions you are taking. Having the trained leaders ready to go will be the difference between success and mediocrity.

Preparing catechists and teachers for the work ahead should be an early element of your pastoral planning. The ten annual sessions of each trimester of *Into the Fields* will help them deepen their communion with God, grow in their knowledge of the faith, and practice the skills needed for effectively implementing a process for lifelong faith formation in the parish. Using *Echoes*, organize it into a similar ten-session format. The group you gather for this may not include all your current catechists or leaders, but it should include the key volunteers who will be responsible for implementing the plan. They will become a vital component and the heartbeat of all you do.

Into the Fields provides a "formation process" much like that experienced in religious life, and it helps fill in that "hole" in the parish that we discussed earlier, by creating a spiritual core of people intentionally growing in their faith and preparing to serve.

6. *Hold a series of meetings over about six months.*

The second major role of the team is the actual planning work itself. The process recommended in *Dreams and Visions* calls for a series of five meetings over the course of about six months. There is no better or worse time of year to begin this process. It's simply best to begin when you are ready. Each meeting will follow a similar format, but with an ever-developing and expanding agenda. The actual meeting agendas are outlined just below, but the general format includes:

✣ Gathering with hospitality

✣ Spending about forty-five minutes in formation yourselves, using one of the *Growing Faith* lessons in each meeting. Use the following method to process the booklets:

• Ask everyone to read it beforehand.

• Move through the booklet from front to back, working on the reflections and exercises which are given for each one.

• Invite members to reflect as well on the artwork, identifying in each picture that element that most strikes them about it.

✣ Next in the meeting, deal with one specific question in the planning process.

✣ Summarize the outcomes and close with social time, including refreshments.

TEAM MEETING AGENDAS

Meeting one: "What are we doing now?"

Suggested Resource: Growing Faith Project: "*The Inborn Hunger for God,*" booklet #1 (which corresponds to articles 26-49 of the *Catechism* or Part 1, Chapter 1 of the *Adult Catechism*). This helps you as a team understand that we humans hunger for God and can know God through the signs and words that God has spoken.

Planning Issue for this meeting: 1) Working through the list of groups above (see the web site for a downloadable worksheet on this), ask yourselves this question: What is the state of each group relative to our Core Work? What do we offer them now? How is what we offer received by members of each group? As you work through these questions, group by group, remember to keep refining your list. For example, as you work with the group, "parents or guardians who have children in religious ed or the school" you may find that you want to break it down a bit more for your purposes into sub groups such as:

+ school parents

+ religious ed parents

+ single parents

+ and so forth

2) The second issue for planning at this meeting is related to this. What have we tried that has succeeded and what have we tried that has failed within each group? What have we done in the past to include each of these groups in our Core Work, which once again, is *to help people deepen their communion with Christ and to sustain that in the church*?

The results of this first meeting are usually very affirming and positive for the parish. Most parishes have many excellent initiatives underway already on which to build toward greatness!

Before you adjourn to refreshments and social time, be sure to consolidate your discussions into a single, brief report. This report and summary should be shared widely in the parish as soon as possible after the meeting.

Meeting Two: "What outcomes do we want to see in the future?"

Suggested Resource: Growing Faith Project: "The Church Passes on Divine Revelation," booklet #3 (which corresponds to articles 74-100 of the *Catechism* or Part 1, Chapter 3 of the *Adult Catechism*). This lays out for your team the historical development of the church, and the sources of revelation that the church hands on: Scripture and Tradition.

Planning issue for this meeting: Having read the material here in *Dreams and Visions*, and knowing what the popes and bishops have been calling us to over the past fifty years, not to mention the insights of your own neighbors and parishioners, identify clearly together what you want to see happen in your parish. (Again, there is a downloadable worksheet for this meeting posted on the web site.) The question on your agenda should read: What outcome do you want to see for each of the affected groups in this parish? What do you want to see happen in the lives of these folks as a result of parish ministry? What do you want people to get from all our efforts as a parish?

Your temptation is to be too general here. But make the list of outcomes for each group quite specific. For example, with "parents who have children in religious ed or the school" you might be tempted to say that you want them to love Christ and be active in the church. Well, okay. Of course you want that. But more specifically, there are other things you want for this group:

✦ To be able to speak articulately about their faith at home

✦ To know how to pray as a household

✦ To be able to understand and pass on the social teachings of the church

✦ And so forth

As you do this work over the coming weeks and months, plan to continually re-visit your desired outcomes to shift them and tweak them until they are downright realistic.

Before you adjourn to refreshments and social time, be sure to consolidate your discussions into a single, brief report. This report and summary should be shared widely in the parish as soon as possible after the meeting.

Meeting Three: "What specific steps should we take to reach our desired outcomes?"

Suggested Resource: Growing Faith Project: "The Mystery of the Church," booklet #17 (which corresponds to articles 748-810 of the *Catechism* or Part 1, Chapter 10 of the *Adult Catechism*). This guides your team to see the deep reality of the church as God's people, the Body of Christ, led by the bishops, and headed by Christ himself.

Planning issue for this meeting: This is a key meeting. In the past two meetings, we have discussed 1) how we've done in the past and 2) what we hope the outcomes to be in the future for each of the groups within the parish. Now it's time to ask this question on your agenda: From the material presented here in *Dreams and Visions,* what elements of the fifth and sixth dimensions of parish ministry can we or should we plan to undertake? Given our parish facilities, our history, the culture of our parish community, and so forth, what specific new programs do we want to offer?

For example, here is a list of some but not all of the various programs discussed in *Dreams and Visions,* building on the documents from the church over the past fifty years:

✢ Parish-based retreats such as Living Christ or Christ Renews His Parish

✢ Other encounters opportunities such as Alpha or RENEW

✢ Faith sharing using the Question of the Week

✛ Formal use of mystagogia in the parish, after ritual experience, work experiences for justice or among the poor, and so forth

✛ Faith Gatherings

✛ Growing-Faith communities

✛ Catechist and teacher formation

✛ And others

In this meeting, as you discuss the various steps you can take to implement *Dreams and Visions*, talking with the pastor and coordinator, choose those elements which you will adopt for your parish, or design others that suit you better. The key here is to set a realistic schedule for implementation. Keep challenging yourself to take those necessary risks needed to succeed at becoming a great parish!

Before you adjourn to refreshments and social time, be sure to consolidate your discussions into a single, brief report. This report and summary should be shared widely in the parish as soon as possible after the meeting.

Meeting Four: "Evaluate what we've done so far"

Suggested Resource: Growing Faith Project: "Who Do People Say That I Am?" booklet #11 (which corresponds to articles 422-483 of the *Catechism* or Part 1, Chapter 7 of the *Adult Catechism*). This helps your team understand more fully who Christ is and how we become disciples ourselves. Of particular help is the "reflection question" on the final spread of the booklet.

Planning issue for this meeting: The purpose of this meeting is twofold. The first is to pause in the planning process and review what you've done so far. Revisit it all step by step.

And in this particular meeting, this is the question for your agenda: How has what we've done so far helped to advance the Core Work of the parish? Have we been too timid, or too ambitious?

The second part of the agenda for this meeting is to talk through those specific programs outlined in the last meeting, revisiting them with an eye to being realistic, yet challenging for the parish. Using the new organizational structure outlined in chapters five, six, and seven of *Dreams and Visions,* how would the new plan for this parish look, drawn and detailed? The pastor and coordinator can assist this part of the agenda by doing some preliminary work before the meeting.

Before you adjourn to refreshments and social time, be sure to consolidate your discussions into a single, brief report. This report and summary should be shared widely in the parish as soon as possible after the meeting.

Meeting Five: "First recommendations"

Suggested Resource: Growing Faith Project: "What Did Christ Teach?" booklet #13 (which corresponds to articles 512-556 of the *Catechism* or Part 1, Chapter 6 of the *Adult Catechism*). This wonderful booklet helps you understand how the teachings of Christ are to be lived in everyday life. It leads you to reflect as a team on how to weave these teachings into the design of your plan.

Planning issue for this meeting: The purpose of this meeting is to hand off to the pastor and coordinator a set of first recommendations, along with that all-important calendar and a sense of the practical aspects of actually carrying it out. Implementing this plan begins immediately, or has most likely already begun. A plan based on dreams and visions in a parish really doesn't have a final form. The planning really doesn't end, and implementing certain parts of the plan can start as soon as they are seen as valuable. In fact, implementing various dimensions of the plan affects future outcomes. As the Core Work of the parish proceeds with more vigor, and as more and more people are in ever deeper communion with Christ and on fire in their hearts, the plan itself changes and shifts. This is driven not by a fixed way of doing things, but by the Spirit, which "blows where it wills."

Therefore, the question on this meeting's agenda might be something like this: For the moment, as a *Dreams and Visions* Team, what do we recommend for the parish? What first steps should we take, or have we already taken?

Before you adjourn to refreshments and social time, be sure to consolidate your discussions into a single, brief report. This report and summary should be shared widely in the parish as soon as possible after the meeting.

Future meetings

Suggested resources: Continue to grow in your own faith at each meeting by using the *Growing Faith Project* booklets.

Planning issues: Once a basic first version of the pastoral plan is written and the calendar is complete, the Team turns its attention to budgets, implementation, monitoring progress, brainstorming to solve problems, and support for the staff and pastor. Continue to meet monthly or bimonthly, and continue to keep the process rolling forward.

7. Prepare a short written pastoral plan document.

Because they must unfold in real time in order to be effective, the format for a written pastoral plan is based on the calendar. No pastoral plan will work that is not calendar-friendly. So as you choose each element to add to the plan, see how it might fit into the parish or school calendar (ignoring the budget for the moment—that will come later). In the end, the plan document you write will be an actual calendar, fleshed out with various offerings. Don't forget this key principle: sometimes when you add new dimensions to your pastoral plan, old ones must be *removed*. I know this can be painful for some folks, but we are in the process of shifting gears as a parish in order to add those two new elements: opportunities for conversion and Faith Gatherings in which to sustain that conversion.

The actual writing of the *Dreams and Visions* Plan for the parish should be done by individuals, not by a team. In preparing the written report of the plan, be sure to keep it brief but complete. You might break down the various ideas into the following categories to help readers get perspective:

✚ major initiatives

✚ minor initiatives

✚ things to stop doing

✚ ideas tabled for now

Under each initiative, it helps readers to know a bit of detail, but use bullets and short descriptions rather than giving every detail. It might be wise to post a complete, detailed report on your parish Web site for those who want to read it, while creating a much shorter version for use in the next step.

8. Invite each affected group to give you feedback.

In order to become a truly great parish, it's necessary to create a culture in which people feel they are being *heard* by the leaders and planners. This is the only way to allow the

Spirit to speak through the community itself. In *Dreams and Visions,* we have been suggesting that you share team meeting reports widely in the parish. We also recommend that you use a series of methods to surface from parish members how they would evaluate various parish programs and offerings. These could be in the form of "dialogue sessions" open to the whole parish. Such a dialogue session might use a process that resembles this:

✛ Start time—determined by the availability of the group. Most will be evenings or weekends, but some may be daytimes.

✛ Begin with breaking open the Word using the Question of the Week.

✛ A *Dreams and Visions* Team member shares about the planned outcomes and the background for them, using the written plans which are gradually being prepared.

✛ Invite the participants to respond using a form of mystagogy: What did you hear here? What touched you? What hopes or fears does this raise in your own heart?

✛ Take careful notes on this feedback, and use the feedback to inform your continuing work. Thus, the Spirit is allowed a voice to help shape your plan.

✛ Share a bit of good food, coffee or wine, and end with a brief prayer. Never skip the food because it's in these moments that the unseen bonds are made among members.

It might also be possible to use some form of a paper survey to uncover how people are responding to the work of the parish. Knowing the results of this can help you direct future work.

ANECDOTAL FEEDBACK

Be especially careful of anecdotal feedback. People who feel disagreeable about things often use phrases such as "No one in the parish really likes this." But who is this person really speaking for? Most of the time, mainly for him or herself or a very small constituency. It's best for such feedback to be given as part of the dialogue session where it can be evaluated by the gathered community.

As you collect feedback, be prepared to hear negative as well as positive input on how the needs of members are being met. In *Good to Great* Jim Collins suggests a fourfold set of basic practices to help you do this. I'm going to paraphrase them here, but the credit goes to Mr. Collins.

✛ First, remember that you are holding these meetings to listen more than to give answers. Therefore, just ask the questions and let the folks do the talking.

✛ Second, the purpose of these meetings is not to "sell" a plan. You want to engage people, and not everyone will share the vision yet. So make this a time of sharing the exciting dreams and visions of the planning team and staff.

✛ Third, when the time comes to talk about past failures in parish life, do so with honesty and kindness, with charity for all. There is no need to establish blame for past failures.

✛ Fourth, hold on to the belief that in the end this will be a truly great parish. At same time, realize that in order to move in that direction, honesty is needed. When this truth is stated, do not ignore it or hide from it.

While dialogue sessions or paper surveys are an important way to communicate and get feedback, other means of communication should also be used, including:

+ The parish bulletin

+ Letter to members of the parish

+ The parish Web site

+ Discussion among leaders not part of the planning team

9. Slowly begin implementing.

In years past, I spent a fair amount of time at a lake cabin in northern Minnesota. We had, on either side of us, neighboring cabins occupied by curious and friendly folks. All three cabins stood quite close to the shore. Once in a while, when there was an east wind, I would inflate a bag full of old beach balls we had on hand. Then, when I knew the neighbors were only watching casually, I'd slowly launch them, one at a time, out into the lake, the gentle winds carrying them to and fro. Eventually there would be as many as a dozen or fifteen bright beach balls bobbing in the surf! It happened so slowly that my neighbors never really saw the drama unfold, until all at once they'd look out into the lake and be surprised to see that I'd done it again!

Launching a pastoral plan such as this one is similar. Start slowly, one beach ball at a time. If you try to launch it all at once, it might be hard to manage. But if you go too slowly, no one will notice. The critical mass of a pastoral plan is the powerful new spirit it instills in the life of the parish. Once that spirit gets flowing, the process of starting up new initiatives is much easier.

We want to build a solid foundation here for the future of the parish, but there will not come a point where you can say to yourself, "Well, good, the planning is done so let's inaugurate the plan." In fact, the planning process is never complete. The Core Work of the parish will never be successfully accomplished, once and for all. In fact, you may do more harm than good by setting a starting date and holding a kick-off celebration. That might work for a building-fund drive, but not for lifelong formation.

Launch your pastoral plan one beach ball at a time!

As I just suggested, there are two possible ways to sabotage the implementation of the plan. The first is by starting too fast, throwing out old programs and replacing them with new ideas that few people understand. People resent losing programs with which they are comfortable and familiar. Wouldn't you? So a gradual start is best, under the guidance of the pastor and coordinator. Simply launch the first beach ball by scheduling the first parish-based retreat, for example, without a lot of fanfare. It only takes a small crew and three rooms. Invite people to it. There's no need to advertise it as a "major new initiative" in the parish. In fact, holding retreats is simply one way we intend to do our Core Work. As the first retreat is being planned, launch another beach ball and plan for the first Faith Gathering, to give those forty new retreatants (and many others) a place to gather to sustain their faith. So begin gradually and without too much fanfare. Simply start launching your initiatives one at a time.

The second way to sabotage this plan is to move too slowly and timidly. If you say to yourself, "Well, okay, yes, this is our Core Work, but we'll only schedule one retreat for this year. And we'll put off the Faith Gatherings until next year." You really aren't launching enough beach balls to be noticed under a plan with this kind of roll out schedule. That might be too slow a start. You really aren't implementing the plan unless you include all the elements that hold it together. Picking and choosing this or that element looks disorganized, and it will be hard for you or anyone in your parish to see any difference from the current situation.

10. Keep doing this forever.

This process goes on forever. We keep finding new and better ways to do our Core Work and to plan and budget for it. Success is in the striving, not the arriving.

What a fantastic period of history this is for the Catholic Church! After nearly seventeen centuries, the popes and bishops, working under the inspiration of the Holy Spirit, have restored the Liturgy and the Catechumenate to full use in the church.

Building on that, and having listened closely to God's people, those same leaders have now set the stage for us to re-invigorate the church by creating opportunities for the same Holy Spirit to touch hearts and lives and deepen communion with God, in the context of parish life through parish-based retreats and other encounters. And we are now planning to do that. How wonderful for the church! We are planning to help folks deepen their communion with Christ.

At the same time, we're planning to provide our people with a simple way to sustain that conversion, through Faith Gatherings for people of all ages and all stages of life. We have the know-how, the people, the will, and the resources to do this with tremendous success.

We do have the ability to follow our dreams and visions for the church, and we do have the ability to choose to become not just good parishes but *great* ones!